ADVANTAGE Grammar

5

Table of Contents

Table of Contents

CREDITS

Concept Development: Kent Publishing Services, Inc.

Written by: Thomas Hatch and Dawn Purney

Editor: Lisa MacCallum

Design/Production: Signature Design Group, Inc.

Art Director: Tom Cochrane

Project Director: Carolea Williams

Introduction

The **Advantage Grammar** series for grades 3-8 offers instruction and practice in key writing skills, including

- grammar and usage
- capitalization and punctuation
- spelling
- writing good sentences
- writing good paragraphs
- editing your work

Take a look at all the advantages this grammar series offers . . .

Strong Skill Instruction

- The teaching component at the top of each lesson provides the support students need to work through the book independently.

- Plenty of skill practice pages will ensure students master essential skills they need to become competent writers.

- Examples, models, and practice activities use content from across the curriculum so students are learning about social studies, science, and literature as they master writing skills.

Editing Your Work pages provide for mixed practice of skills in a format that supports today's process approach to the teaching of writing.

Take a Test Drive pages provide practice using a test-taking format such as those included in national standardized and proficiency tests.

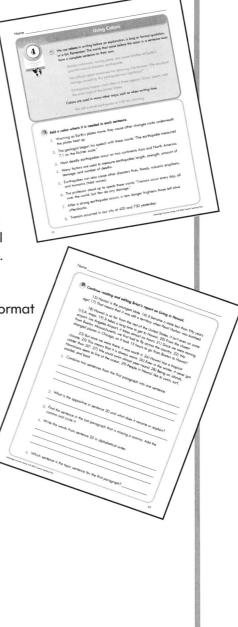

LESSON

1

CHANGING EARTH

Understanding Verb Tense

Verb tenses indicate when the action in a sentence happens. There are three main verb tenses.

past tense: We **built** the wall.
present tense: We **build** the wall.
future tense: We **will build** the wall again.

For regular verbs, simply add *-ed* or *-d* to form the past tense.

climb—The goat **climbed** the mountain.

Irregular verbs do not form the past tense by adding *-ed* or *-d*. Each irregular verb has its own set of rules to form the past tense.

grow—One tall birch tree **grew** on the mountain.

A **Circle the tense of the bold verb in each sentence.**

1. He **studies** erosion as part of his geography class.

   past   present   future

2. The wind **eroded** my sandcastle this morning.

   past   present   future

3. The grasses **look** nice on the shore.

   past   present   future

4. People **planted** grasses on the shoreline.

   past   present   future

5. The plants' roots **will help** the soil stay in place.

   past   present   future

6. He **proved** that his theory of erosion was correct.

   past   present   future

7. After enough time, however, even the rocks **will erode**, too.

   past   present   future

8. Plants **grow** when they receive enough sunlight.

   past   present   future

B Complete the chart with the correct form for each verb. Some verbs are irregular verbs.

Present Tense	Past Tense	Future Tense
	flew	
form		
	grew	
		will walk
	asked	
		will see
	washed	
	knew	

C Find the past and present tense verbs in the word search. Write each verb under its correct tense.

H	A	B	M	X	S	O	A
W	A	L	K	L	A	N	S
A	K	E	S	A	W	E	K
S	I	W	C	T	A	R	P
H	L	A	F	L	Y	N	S
E	A	R	O	R	S	N	E
D	T	G	R	E	W	B	E
V	I	U	M	Z	Q	P	A

Present

_____

_____

_____

_____

_____

Past

_____

_____

_____

_____

Name _____

2

CHANGING
EARTH

Understanding Verb Tense

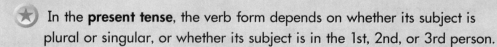

⭐ In the **present tense**, the verb form depends on whether its subject is plural or singular, or whether its subject is in the 1st, 2nd, or 3rd person.

- Plural subject:
  The goats **walk** up the mountainside.

- Singular subject: add -*s* or -*es* to the verb.
  The goat **walks** up the mountainside.

- 1st person:
  I **walk** up the mountainside.

- 2nd person:
  You **walk** up the mountainside.

- 3rd person: add -*s* or -*es* to the verb.
  He **walks** up the mountainside.

A **Circle the verb in the parentheses that best completes the sentence.**

1. Volcanic eruptions (form, forms) the Cascade Mountains.

2. The lava (cool, cools) slowly.

3. Volcanoes (build, builds) the Hawaiian Islands.

4. The mountains in Hawaii seem to (rise, rises) into the sky.

5. Water (erode, erodes) away the weaker rocks.

6. The river (wears, wear) away the land of the Black Hills.

7. Likewise, the Colorado River (create, creates) the Grand Canyon.

8. Oceans and lakes do (shape, shapes) the land.

Advantage Grammar Grade 5 © 2005 Creative Teaching Press

Name _____

B Write a sentence about our planet using one of the tenses: past, present, or future.

_____

_____

C Complete each sentence using a form of the word in bold to make the sentence past, present, or future tense. On the line following the sentence, name the tense you used.

tread 1. He _____ upon Earth's crust. _____

blow 2. The force of the eruption _____ off the top of Mt. St. Helens. _____

move 3. Each plate _____ slowly across Earth's molten layer. _____

cause 4. At times, the movement _____ earthquakes or volcanic eruptions. _____

form 5. Sometimes mountains _____ when plates meet. _____

have 6. When plates met, they _____ nowhere to go but up! _____

burst 7. The river _____ its steep banks. _____

fall 8. The rock climber _____ during the earthquake. _____

bend 9. Some rock actually _____ without breaking. _____

make 10. Other times, the great force _____ the plates buckle. _____

Name _____

Simple and Compound Sentences

 A complete sentence has a **subject** (noun or pronoun) and **predicate** (verb or verb phrase).

Ice forms quickly. The cold temperature makes water freeze.
subject predicate   subject   predicate

A **sentence fragment** is not a complete sentence—it is missing a subject or a predicate. For example:

An ice-cold glacier.   Grows gradually over time.
subject   predicate

A phrase that contains a subject and a predicate is also called a **clause**. If a sentence has more than one clause, it is called a **compound sentence**.

Ice builds up, and   it becomes a glacier.
subject predicate   subject   predicate
     clause   clause

The difference between a simple sentence and a compound sentence is that a compound sentence has two clauses.

A glacier in the sea is called an iceberg.   A glacier covers the South Pole, but

    Simple sentence   an iceberg covers the North Pole.

                                                       Compound sentence

A Underline the subject and circle the predicate of each sentence. Cross out any sentence fragments.

1. A glacier is formed by snow, ice, air, and dirt.

2. Snowflakes and snow grains.

3. Packed snow slowly becomes ice.

4. Some glaciers are ice sheets.

5. Ice sheets covered the land completely.

B **Draw a line between the two clauses. Underline each subject and circle each predicate.**

1. Glaciers occur in polar regions or high altitudes, because they are cold.

2. Part of a glacier sometimes breaks off, and then it forms an iceberg.

3. Sometimes a glacier fills a valley between mountains, so it is called a valley glacier.

4. Part of the glacier is melting, and another part is freezing.

5. Sometimes part of the glacier covers the land, yet another part floats in the ocean.

C **Label each simple sentence SS and each compound sentence CS. Draw a line between the clauses in the compound sentences.**

1. ____ Glaciers move, but they move very slowly.

2. ____ The leading edge of the glacier is called the nose or snout.

3. ____ The glacier nose picks up loose dirt and rocks.

4. ____ Glaciers pick up debris in one place and deposit it in another.

5. ____ Deposited glacial debris formed the Cape Cod peninsula.

6. ____ Some glaciers carve out large bowls in the land, and the ice melts into the bowls.

7. ____ Long ago, glaciers created the Great Lakes.

8. ____ The heavy glaciers smooth over the land underneath them.

9. ____ Ice that doesn't melt for a season is not yet a glacier, but it is on its way!

10. ____ Glaciers form over a period of about 1,000 years.

LESSON 4

CHANGING EARTH

Using Colons

⭐ We use **colons** in writing before an explanation, a long or formal quotation, or a list. Remember: The words that come before the colon in a sentence must form a complete sentence on their own.

Besides volcanoes, moving plates also cause another of Earth's greatest natural disasters: earthquakes.

The official report contained the following information: "The structural damage caused by the earthquake was significant."

Earthquakes happen most often in three regions: China, Japan, and the west coast of the United States.

Colons are used in many other ways, such as when writing time.

We felt a small earthquake at 9:30 this morning.

A Add a colon where it is needed in each sentence.

1. Warning as Earth's plates move, they cause other changes rocks underneath the plates heat up.

2. The geologist began his speech with these words "The earthquake measured 7.1 on the Richter scale."

3. Most deadly earthquakes occur on two continents Asia and North America.

4. Many factors are used to measure earthquakes length, strength, amount of damage, and number of deaths.

5. Earthquakes can also cause other disasters fires, floods, volcanic eruptions, and tsunamis (tidal waves).

6. The professor stood up to speak these words "Tremors occur every day, all over the world, but few do any damage."

7. After a strong earthquake occurs, a new danger frightens those left alive aftershocks.

8. Tremors occurred in our city at 400 and 730 yesterday.

Colons are also used in E-mail and at the end of the greeting in a business letter.

From: Gram <earthmover@sfca.com>
To: Jacob <tremor@ethquk.com>
Subject: Saturday
Date: Sat, Oct 16, 2004 10:15

Dear Mr. Jones:
We wish to inform you that your subscription has expired.

Colons separate titles from subtitles.

Aftershock: Earthquake in New York

B Add colons where they are needed in this E-mail.

From Jacob <tremor@ ethquk.com>
To <programming@infotv.com>
Subject movie times
Date Mon, Sept 6, 2004 4 36

Dear Programming Department

I watched Channel 5 on Friday night and saw the end of "San Francisco Aftermath of an Earthquake." It was a very interesting movie. Please tell me when your channel will air it again, so I can watch the entire movie.

Sincerely yours,
Jacob Kersh

 Write a reply from the programming department to Jacob's E-mail. Use colons where needed.

From <programming@infotv.com>
To Jacob <tremor@ethquk.com>
Subject Re movie times
Date

_____

_____

Name _____

Informational Paragraphs

⭐ Informational paragraphs often start with a topic sentence that tells the main idea. They follow this structure:

Topic sentence—One sentence stating the main idea. It usually comes first.
Supportive sentences—Sentences giving supporting details about the main idea.
Closing sentence—A restatement of, or something more about, the main idea. This sentence is optional.

In this paragraph, the topic and closing sentences are underlined. The other sentences are supportive sentences.

<u>A river changes the land through which it flows.</u> Over time, the water wears down its channel, which is the land beneath and around the river. Then, the riverbed cuts deeper and deeper into the earth. The sides get steeper. Eventually a cliff, gorge, or canyon is made. When a river floods, it often finds a shortcut to a section downstream. If the river's old path is cut off from the new channel, it forms a pond. <u>A river reshapes the land, from its source to the mouth.</u>

A Read the paragraph below. Underline the topic and closing sentences, and circle the supportive sentences.

Rapids form when the riverbed slopes more steeply downhill. The river deposits many of its larger rocks on these slopes. As the water breaks over the rocky riverbed, foam or white water appears. Because white water moves more quickly, many people like to raft in the rapids. Besides the boulders, rapids often have waterfalls and a strong undertow, which pulls objects below the surface. Although they may be thrilling, rapids are also more dangerous.

B Write your own informational paragraph about rivers on another sheet of paper. Be sure your paragraph contains a topic sentence, supporting details, and a closing sentence.

Name _____

Paragraphs can also be organized around a sequence—a list of things that happen in order. Each sentence gives a piece of information or a step organized according to when it happened or when it should happen.

Words like these guide the reader through the steps:
first   next   then   eventually   finally

C **Read the paragraph. Then, number the sentences in chronological order. Look for time-order words to help you.**

A river always starts at a source. The source may be a lake on a hill or just a trickle of melting snow from a mountaintop. First, the river flows downhill. Then, more water joins it. Next, other streams, called tributaries, flow into the river. Then, the river widens. Eventually, the river flows into a lake or an ocean. This is called the river's mouth.

_____ Waterfalls change the land around them over time.

_____ Eventually, the splashes erode the soft rock behind the waterfall.

_____ First, the falling water hits the surface below.

_____ Then, it splashes up against the rocks.

_____ Next, the water erodes the hard rock underneath the waterfall.

D **Write a paragraph that has a chronological order. It can tell a short story or give instructions on how to do something. Your paragraph should have three or more steps.**

_____

_____

_____

_____

_____

_____

Name _____

Spelling the *sh* sound

 Some sounds in English are spelled in many different ways: *sh*, *su*, *ci*, *ti*, and *si* all can make the *sh* sound. For example, the *sh* sound in the word *glacier* is spelled *ci*.

A **Read the essay Jordan wrote. Circle the words that have the *sh* sound in them.**

In social studies, we learned about ways the earth changes. One kind of change is erosion, which is the wearing away of the land by natural causes, such as the weather. After nature, man is the biggest factor in changing the land. This would not be a natural cause, but an artificial one.

Some ways that people change the earth are good, but a lot of this change is not good. Usually it is commercial businesses that hurt the earth. These companies want financial gain, and they don't seem to think about the land. Mining companies dig deep holes looking for minerals and precious gems. On occasion, they don't cover the holes or plant new seeds to replace the plants they dug up. Other organizations are not cautious about their pollution. They make the air and water dirty, as well as the land. It is a shame these people don't appreciate the earth more.

Unfortunately, our cities also damage the earth. Trees are torn down, and fields are covered with cement.

Many governments now try to control what people can do to the earth. Sometimes they make laws, but sometimes they can only make suggestions for companies to follow. This causes tension around the nation, because some people think the government should protect the earth.

B Write the words you circled in the essay in the correct category. Then add other words you know that spell the *sh* sound the same way.

sh	su	ci	ti	si
_____	_____	_____	_____	_____
_____	_____	_____	_____	_____
_____	_____	_____	_____	_____
_____	_____	_____	_____	_____
_____	_____	_____	_____	_____
_____	_____	_____	_____	_____
_____	_____	_____	_____	_____
_____	_____	_____	_____	_____
_____	_____	_____	_____	_____
_____	_____	_____	_____	_____

C Write a short informational paragraph about pollution using as many *sh* sound words as you can.

_____

_____

_____

_____

_____

_____

_____

Name _____

Editing Your Work

 Editing your work is an important step in the writing process. Many tests ask you to show what you know about editing.

 Alexis wrote a report about volcanoes. Help her analyze and edit her work. Read the first two paragraphs and follow the directions.

Volcanoes

1) Most people think of volcanoes as being bad, but really, volcanoes change the earth in both good and bad ways. 2) For example, none of the Hawaiian Islands would exist if it weren't for volcanoes! 3) The ashes make the ground very good for plants to grow. 4) After an erupshon, the ash in the sky makes something beautiful a sunset. 5) Some people even use volcanic rocks in their buildings.

6) Volcanoes are classified two different ways: by shape or by activity level. 7) Scientists name three main shapes of volcanoes, but they know several other shapes that are more unusual. 8) If a volcano is active it causes earthquakes, moves the earth, releases lava or gases, or erupts. 9) Scientist call a volcano dormant if it has erupted in the past but is not currently active. 10) If a volcano has not erupted in recorded history, it is considered extinct. 11) Sometimes scientists find out they are wrong about an extinct volcano, because it erupts!

1. What is the topic sentence of the first paragraph? _____
_____

2. Sentence 4 has two errors. Rewrite the sentence correctly.

_____

_____

3. What is the topic sentence of the second paragraph?

_____

4. Find the compound sentence in the second paragraph. Draw a line between the clauses, then underline both subjects and circle both predicates.

Name _____

B **Read Alexis' account of a famous volcanic eruption. Then answer the questions to help her revise and edit her work.**

1) On March 16, 1980, a series of earthquakes began, lasting for weeks. 2) After a few days, a steam exploshon blew the ice cap off the top of the mountain. 3) It created a crater, but the crater soon cracked into many pieces. 4) During that time, the north side of the mountain swelled outward. 5) At 832 AM on May 18, a huge earthquake shook the swollen part. 6) The entire top of the mountain became a landslide. 7) Then the volcano erupted.

8) An hour later another eruption happened. 9) When hot rocks and gas melted the snow on the mountain, the water combined with the rocks and lava, and a mudflow was born. 10) The volcanic mudflow poured down the mountain doing much damage it destroyed roads and bridges and ripped trees from their roots. 11) That afternoon, avalanches of hot ash, gas, and rock started falling. 12) Because there was so much ash in the air, the sky was completely dark for hundreds of miles around the mountain.

13) Since then, smaller eruptions and earthquakes have shaped and reshaped the mountain. 14) Mt. St. Helens is still active and dangerous.

1. In the first paragraph, a word with the *sh* sound is misspelled. Write the word correctly here. _____

2. What other words in the passage have the *sh* sound?
    _____

3. Which sentence in the first paragraph is a compound sentence? _____

4. Sentence 5 has an error. Rewrite the sentence correctly.
    _____

5. Rewrite sentence 10 to make it two complete sentences.
    _____

6. Write one past tense verb from the essay.
    _____

Take a Test Drive

8

Fill in the bubble beside the correct answer.

Dylan wrote an essay about how weather changes the earth. Help him analyze and edit his essay. Read the essay and answer the questions that follow.

1) The weather can change the earth. 2) Most people think only of extreme weather, such as floods and tornadoes, as something that would change the land. 3) But everyday weather can, too. 4) It takes a lot longer, however, for rain to change a hillside than it would take a flood. 5) These are common kinds of weather in the United States rain, snow, winds, and even sunshine.

6) Snow can change the land around it. 7) For example, snow may fall and then melt a little. 8) The melted snow slips into tiny holes in the ground. 9) But then the melted snow freezes and it becomes ice. 10) Ice takes up more room than water does, so it pushes the dirt around it. 11) This movement creates cracks in the earth! 12) In cold areas, snow does the same thing to cement sidewalks and roads.

1. Which statement is true about sentence 1?
  Ⓐ It is a compound sentence.
  Ⓑ "The weather" is the predicate part of the sentence.
  Ⓒ The verb *can* is in the future tense.
  Ⓓ The word *change* is a regular verb.

2. How should sentence 5 be changed?
  Ⓕ Spell the word *sunshine* correctly as *sunciine*
  Ⓖ Add a colon after the word *weather*.
  Ⓗ Add a colon after the word *States*.
  Ⓙ Change nothing—it is correct.

3. Which statement is false?
  Ⓐ The second paragraph is organized in chronological, or time, order.
  Ⓑ In sentence 6, the word *snow* is the subject.
  Ⓒ Sentence 7 is a compound sentence.
  Ⓓ Sentence 11 is a simple sentence.

Advantage Grammar Grade 5 © 2005 Creative Teaching Press

Name _____

Dylan's class recorded the weather at their school for a local television station. Read and edit Dylan's E-mail report to the station manager.

Subject: Grant School weather report
From: Mrs. M <Mrsmsclass@gs.edu>
To: Mr. Dailey <weathercenter@yournews.com>
Date: Mon, Jan 10, 2005 9:47 AM

Dear Mr. Dailey,

1) We checked the weather at 840 this morning. 2) The temperature was 39 degrees. 3) The wind speed was 10 miles per hour.

4) Thank you for mentioning our school in the news commercial last night. 5) We always watch your stashon and we think you're the best!

Dylan

4. Which statement is true about sentence 1?
Ⓕ "We checked" is the subject of the sentence.
Ⓖ The time (8:40) needs a colon.
Ⓗ "The temperature" is the subject of the sentence.
Ⓙ A colon should be added after the word *temperature*.

5. Which word spells the *sh* sound correctly?
Ⓐ checked   Ⓒ commercial
Ⓑ temperature   Ⓓ stashon

6. Which verb is irregular?
Ⓕ checked   Ⓗ mentioning
Ⓖ watch   Ⓙ think

7. Which statement is false about sentence 5?
Ⓐ It is a compound sentence.
Ⓑ The word *we* is the subject.
Ⓒ A colon needs to be added after the word *stashon*.
Ⓓ The words *watch* and *think* are the predicates in the sentence.

8. Which sentence is the topic sentence for the first paragraph?
Ⓕ sentence 1
Ⓖ sentence 2
Ⓗ sentence 3
Ⓙ There is no topic sentence.

Name _____

Understanding Verb Tense

 The **progressive form** indicates ongoing action. To form the present progressive tense, use the correct form of the verb *to be* plus the *–ing* form of the second verb.

I **am talking** about our founding fathers.
She **is talking** about our founding fathers.
They **are talking** about our founding fathers.

To form the past progressive tense, use the past tense form of the verb *to be* plus the *-ing* form of the second verb.

Each Pilgrim **was standing** at the water's edge.

People on the *Mayflower* **were building** the first permanent settlement in the new land.

A **Underline each progressive tense verb. Label the sentence PAST for past progressive or PRESENT for present progressive.**

_____ 1. Two ships left for the New World, but the boat the *Speedwell*, was leaking too much to continue.

_____ 2. Both ships were returning to England.

_____ 3. The *Mayflower* could not dock where the crew was planning to settle.

_____ 4. The settlers were living on the boat until they found a new place to live.

_____ 5. I am settling in a new area, which is now called Plymouth, Massachusetts.

_____ 6. I am finding that the Pilgrims lived a very difficult life.

_____ 7. She is learning about who wrote the "Mayflower Compact."

_____ 8. The Pilgrims were creating one of the first settlements in the New World!

⭐ The **emphatic form** is used to stress certainty or place emphasis on a verb. The emphatic tense is formed with the verbs *do*, *does*, or *did* plus the present tense of the second verb.

Squanto provided help to the Pilgrims. → Squanto **did provide** help to the Pilgrims.

B **Write the emphatic form of the verb in the blank.**

survived　**1.** Only half of the settlers _____ the long winter.

served　**2.** William Bradford _____ as governor of the colony.

tried　**3.** The settlers _____ to farm before the natives taught them how.

believe　**4.** I _____ that people already lived in the New World.

shared　**5.** The Native Americans _____ the land with the people from England.

C **Write two sentences about the New World using the progressive verb form and two sentences using the emphatic verb form.**

_____

_____

_____

_____

_____

_____

_____

LESSON

10

EUROPEAN COLONIES IN AMERICA

Commonly Misused Words

⭐ Sometimes we use the wrong word because it sounds or looks similar to the correct word.

> Because corn grew in America long ago, the Native Americans were able to enjoy popcorn for desert.

The correct noun is *dessert*; the word *desert* means, "a very dry place."

Most verbs have several forms, so it's easy to make mistakes about which form to use in a sentence.

> Before the explorers gone to America, they traveled to other lands.

The word *went* is the correct verb; *gone* and *went* are both past tense forms of *go*, but *went* is correct here.

Ⓐ **Circle the verb that best completes the sentence.**

1. Because they thought they _____ in India, the explorers called the natives "Indians."

   be   were   was   is

2. One explorer kidnapped several natives and _____ them back to Europe.

   bring   take   brought   brung

3. One famous native was called Tisquantum. You have probably heard of him, _____ you know him as "Squanto."

   accept   except

4. In England, Tisquantum could _____ been sold as a slave, but some priests bought his freedom.

   have   of   would   had

5. After a few trips, Tisquantum was let _____ and returned to his people.

   lost   loose   lose   loss

          Advantage Grammar Grade 5 © 2005 Creative Teaching Press

Name _____

B **Use a word from the box to complete each sentence.**

saw	sore	scene	seen	leave	leaf	your
you're	there	they're	their	its	it's	lay	lie

1. The explorers _____ animals and plants they had never seen before.

2. One lady was _____ falling overboard.

3. Although they wanted to, many Pilgrims couldn't _____ the New World.

4. The anchor tore loose from _____ mooring.

5. Many explorers died because the sickness spread quickly throughout _____ close quarters.

6. Run over _____ and pick up that book about "The Mayflower."

7. Many Pilgrims didn't believe the strange _____ before their eyes.

8. By the first Thanksgiving, _____ were only four women still alive.

9. The settlers told the captain, " _____ welcome to stay as long as you want."

10. _____ not surprising that the captain didn't stay.

Sentence Fragments and Run-on Sentences

⭐ A **sentence fragment** is an incomplete sentence. A fragment is usually missing a subject or a predicate.

Although not always by choice, many <u>colonies</u>.

Ruled these countries by force.

Colonies is the subject, there is no predicate

Ruled is the predicate, there is no subject.

Transitive verbs take an object. If a verb is transitive, it must have an object or the sentence will also be a fragment.

In 1947, England granted.
sentence fragment

In 1947, England granted independence to India.
complete sentence

 A **Read the sentences. If the sentence is complete, write *S*. If it is a sentence fragment, write *F*.**

____ **1.** A colony is a group that settles far from home but is still ruled by its homeland.

____ **2.** Taken over and ruled by another country.

____ **3.** In ancient times, the aggressive Roman Empire.

____ **4.** Some Romans offered the natives all the rights of a Roman citizen.

____ **5.** The Pilgrim's heavy loads.

____ **6.** The settlers would not always bring.

____ **7.** It was not long before they had met.

____ **8.** Some colonies made the natives.

____ **9.** Drains the money supply of the ruling government.

____ **10.** Modern colonies brought about.

Run-on sentences have clauses that are not connected properly or are simply too long.

People wanting religious freedom started the Plymouth colony but most of those who started the Jamestown colony were the kinds of people who wanted an adventure or a higher income instead of religious freedom.

The easiest way to fix a run-on sentence is to insert a period after the first clause, then begin a new sentence. Rewrite to eliminate unnecessary wordiness.

People wanting religious freedom started the Plymouth colony. However, people wanting an adventure and a higher income started the Jamestown colony.

B Rewrite each run-on sentence as two or more complete sentences.

1. In 1607, English businessmen sailed to what is now Virginia to settle there, and there they would look for gold and other riches they had heard were in this "New World."

   _____

   _____

2. The settlers looked for a place that would be easy to defend from other gold-diggers, so they sailed up a river to find a beautiful, secure area of land large enough to hold all 104 men.

   _____

   _____

3. Although the land was good for defense, the Jamestown settlement had other problems, for example, mosquitoes passed deadly diseases to the men.

   _____

   _____

4. Also, natives often attacked the settlers, and finally, some settlers could not—or would not—hunt for food.

   _____

   _____

Name _____

Using Quotation Marks

 A **quotation** is a person's exact words or thoughts. Quotation marks surround the words of the speaker.

End punctuation follows these rules:
- Commas and periods go inside the final quotation marks.
- Semicolons and colons go outside the final quotation marks.
- Question marks and exclamation points go inside the final quotation marks if the end punctuation is part of the quotation. If not, place the question mark or exclamation point outside the final quotation marks.

Use a comma after an introductory expression.

When the Jamestown settlers would not hunt, Captain John Smith said, "He that will not work, shall not eat."

 Add the correct punctuation to each sentence.

1. Benjamin Franklin spoke of actions being better than words when he said Well done is better than well said.

2. Although he led the military in the Revolutionary War, George Washington himself stated My first wish is to see this plague of mankind, war, banished from the earth.

3. Patrick Henry spoke the first declaration of independence when he said Give me liberty or give me death!

4. As the colonies decided to fight for their independence, Thomas Paine said These are the times that try men's souls.

5. The great Thomas Jefferson once said Friendship is precious, not only in the shade, but in the sunshine of life.

6. British writer Samuel Johnson stated Hope is necessary in every condition.

7. Early American poet Anne Bradstreet wrote If we had no winter, the spring would not be so pleasant.

Name _____

 Sometimes a person's exact words are part of a longer sentence. A quotation can also begin a sentence.

Use a comma to end a quote when it is:
- followed by a concluding expression.

   "Knowledge is of two kinds," wrote Samuel Johnson. "We know a subject ourselves, or we know where we can find information on it."

- followed by an interrupting expression. In this case, also use a comma after the interrupting expression.

   "The British War has left us in debt," said Thomas Jefferson, "but that is a cheap price for the good it has done us."

B **Add the correct punctuation to each sentence.**

1. I'm a great believer in luck said Thomas Jefferson. I find the harder I work, the more I have of it

2. There never was a good knife made of bad steel Ben Franklin wrote.

3. Take care that you never spell a word wrong Thomas Jefferson once told his daughter. Always before you write a word, consider how it is spelled, and, if you do not remember, turn to a dictionary

4. Men are born to succeed, not fail Henry David Thoreau said.

5. We are inclined to believe those whom we do not know because they have never deceived us said Samuel Johnson

C **Write a conversation between two people using quotations.**

_____

_____

_____

13

EUROPEAN
COLONIES
IN AMERICA

Spelling Words with Silent Letters

 Some words in English use irregular spelling, such as silent letters.

The first English colonists settled on Roanoke **Island**, off the coast of North Carolina.

Everyone **knows** how the Roanoke Colony began, but not much is **known** about its ending.

 Read each sentence aloud. Find words with silent letters and underline the silent letters.

1. In 1585, years before Plymouth or Jamestown, English families sailed to a small isle off the coast of what is now North Carolina.

2. Governor Lane would take charge of the settlement.

3. They arrived in autumn—too late to plant new crops.

4. Native Americans sometimes taught the colonists how to farm the land.

5. When the natives didn't help them, the settlers kidnapped the natives or stole from them.

6. Soon the islanders would be at war.

7. When a ship came from England, the settlers returned with it, although 15 men from the boat stayed behind.

8. No one knows what the men did among the palms, for when the ship returned, they had disappeared.

9. Colonists on this ship were talked into staying, but they too disappeared.

10. Some believe the Roanoke settlers moved inland with the other natives, and some believe the natives killed the settlers.

    Advantage Grammar Grade 5 © 2005 Creative Teaching Press

Name _____

 In English, some letters can create more than one sound. Besides the consonant *y* sound in *yet*, *y* makes the long *i* sound at the end of many one-syllable words.

> The Native Americans were not **shy** with the new settlers.

At the end of longer words, *y* makes the *long e* sound.

> Roanoke Island was a **lovely** place.

In the middle of words, *y* makes the *short i* sound.

> The early settlers found the **rhythm** of the ocean waves soothing.

B Underline the words with *y* and write them in the correct column according to their sound. Then add other words to each column.

1. Roanoke is known as the Lost Colony.

2. The lost settlement of Roanoke is one no one has been able to solve yet.

3. The story of the Roanoke settlers is still mysterious.

4. Many people have written about it—some even in rhyme.

consonant *y*	long *e*	long *i*	short *i*

Name _____

Topic and Supporting Sentences

14

EUROPEAN
COLONIES
IN AMERICA

⭐ All supportive sentences in a paragraph should further explain the main idea in the topic sentence. The topic sentence is underlined in the following example.

> English explorers established several colonies in the New World. Best known are the thirteen colonies that gained independence as the United States of America. The English also fought the French over parts of what became Canada. In fact, one province in Canada is called British Columbia. Many British settlers also enjoyed the tropical colonies of the Caribbean islands. Other English settlers moved into the Northwest Territory, which was later broken into the U.S. states, such as Ohio.

A **Read the paragraph below. Underline the topic sentence.**

Many French explorers also settled parts of North America. They had many forts in areas that are now called Pennsylvania, Michigan, Louisiana, and New York. The French also controlled a large part of eastern Canada until the British took control at the end of the French and Indian War. Like the British, many French settlers enjoyed living on islands in the Caribbean.

Now place a check next to the sentence that would best fit the paragraph.

____ The French also had many colonies in Africa.

____ Spanish explorers were the first to settle in the Florida area.

____ The French explored North America; some returned home.

B **Write your own paragraph about the New World. Be sure your paragraph contains a topic sentence and supporting ideas.**

_____

_____

_____

Advantage Grammar Grade 5 © 2005 Creative Teaching Press

C Read the paragraph below. Underline the topic sentence. Draw a line through the sentence that does not give supporting details about the main idea.

Spanish explorers also built colonies across North America. Mexico, as well as parts of Texas and California, were first explored and claimed for Spain. Spanish settlers built over 200 cities in the United States. The Spanish controlled most of Central America at one time. The Spanish army was the colonists' ally during the Revolutionary War. Spanish influences can still be seen in the United States—especially in the Southwest.

Now place a check next to the sentence that would best fit the paragraph.

____ The British tried to take over the Spanish fort in Florida, St. Augustine.

____ These influences include food, language, music, and architecture.

____ Spanish settlers lived in islands in the Caribbean, such as Cuba and Puerto Rico.

D Read the paragraph below. Underline the topic sentence. Draw a line through the sentence that does not give supporting details about the main idea.

People from many countries moved to America when it was first discovered. Swedish settlers began in Delaware. Pennsylvania had pockets of Germans, Irish, as well as British. Not all the new settlers started their own colonies; many settled in areas established by people from other countries. Native Americans sometimes shared the land and sometimes chased out new settlers.

Now place a check next to the sentence that would best fit the paragraph.

____ Meriwether Lewis and William Clark explored the American Northwest.

____ People from Northern European countries, such as Denmark and Holland, also moved to America.

____ Anyone living in North or South America could be called Americans.

Name _____

Editing Your Work

 Editing your work is an important step in the writing process. Many tests ask you to show what you know about editing.

 Zack wrote an essay about the Northwest Territory. Help him analyze and edit his work. Read Zack's essay and follow the directions.

The Northwest Territory

1) The Northwest Territory was born when families moved west of the colonies to start they're own settlements. 2) The places they settled were becoming what is now Ohio, Michigan, Indiana, Illinois, Wisconsin, and parts of Minnesota. 3) Soon the settlements became towns and then, later, some towns became cities. 4) The French had already given up their claim to any part of the land after the French and Indian War. 5) By 1787, the colonies officially made a new territory called the Old Northwest. 6) But Henry David Thoreau said What is most interesting for the history of the Northwest are the natural facts, which are with out date.

1. Which sentence has a progressive verb tense? Write the sentence number and the progressive tense verbs.

   _____

2. Which sentence is a run-on sentence? Rewrite it here as two sentences.

   _____

   _____

3. In which sentence is *there/their/they're* used incorrectly? Write the sentence number and the word that should replace the incorrect homophone.

   _____

4. Rewrite sentence 6 using correct punctuation. _____

   _____

B Continue reading and editing Zack's essay.

7) When it became an official territory, the Northwest Territory was given a governor and judges. 8) If any part of the territory gained 60,000 people, it could than become a state.

9) Even though it already had cities, people in the colonies thought of the territory as being dense woods full of wild natives. 10) In fact, British writer Doris Lessing described the northwest as "very far away, dark forests full of barbarians whom these people scarcely accounted as human at all". 11) Although not barbarians, the natives did not like the new settlers. 12) Often a struggle was going on for the land.

1. List the words with silent letters in sentence 8. _____
   _____

2. Circle the incorrect word in sentence 8. Write the word that should replace it.
   _____
   _____

3. Find the sentence that has a progressive tense. Write the sentence number and the progressive verb.
   _____

4. Underline the topic sentence in the second paragraph.

5. Check the sentence below that would best fit at the begining of the second paragraph.

   ____ New settlers eventually forced out the natives in the Northwest Territory.

   ____ Fur traders also lived and worked in this area.

   ____ The territory was the area east of the Mississippi River, and between the Ohio River and the Great Lakes.

Name _____

16

EUROPEAN
COLONIES
IN AMERICA

Take a Test Drive

Fill in the bubble beside the correct answer.

Emily listed interesting facts about the European colonies in America. Help her analyze and edit her facts. Read the facts and answer the questions that follow.

1) **Virginia** was the first place the English tried to settle. 2) At first, the entire coast of North America was called Virginia.

3) **Massachusetts** included what is now Massachusetts and Maine, yet New Hampshire was between them. 4) Massachusetts did not lose Maine until Maine became it's own state in 1820.

5) **New Hampshire** also part of Massachusetts—sometimes. 6) First new settlements were joining with Massachusetts. 7) Then England made them separate, then joined them again, then finally separated them again. 8) England could not leave them alone!

9) **Rhode Island**, as everyone knows, is the smallest state and was the smallest colony. 10) It was begun when a minister from Massachusetts moved there to start his own church.

1. Which word contains a *y* that does NOT spell the long *e* sound?
Ⓐ colony
Ⓒ yet
Ⓑ finally
Ⓓ everyone

2. Which statement is true about sentence 4?
Ⓕ It is a run-on sentence.
Ⓖ The contraction *it's* should be replaced with the possessive word *its*.
Ⓗ There aren't any silent letters in the sentence.
Ⓙ It is a supporting detail about the main idea in sentence 1.

3. Which sentence uses the progressive tense?
Ⓐ sentence 1
Ⓒ sentence 5
Ⓑ sentence 2
Ⓓ sentence 6

4. Which statement is NOT true about sentence 5?
Ⓕ It is a sentence fragment.
Ⓗ It has an emphatic verb in it.
Ⓖ There are two silent *e's* in the sentence.
Ⓙ It is a topic sentence.

Continue reading and editing Emily's facts.

11) **North Carolina's** first settlement, Roanoke, was started by Sir Walter Raleigh, who, besides being an adventurer, he was also a poet. 12) One line from one of his poems says, "Who desires to know what will be hereafter, let him think of what is past." 13) Raleigh only lived at the colony for one year.

14) **New Jersey** started as a colony called New Sweden. 15) Than it became part of New Netherland, which became New York.

16) **Georgia** was first explored and settled by the Spanish. 18) The English and Spanish were fighting over the land for almost one hundred years!

19) **Connecticut** is a Native American word meaning "long river".

5. Which statement is true about sentence 11?
   Ⓐ It is a sentence fragment.
   Ⓑ It is a run-on sentence.
   Ⓒ It has a progressive verb in it.
   Ⓓ The letter *y* in *by* makes the long *e* sound.

6. Which sentence does *not* belong in the paragraph about North Carolina?
   Ⓕ sentence 11
   Ⓖ sentence 12
   Ⓗ sentence 13
   Ⓙ None—all of the sentences belong in the paragraph.

7. How should sentence 15 be changed?
   Ⓐ Change the word *than* to *then*.
   Ⓑ Change the word *became* to *become*.
   Ⓒ Add a silent *k* at the beginning of the word *New*.
   Ⓓ It should not be changed at all.

8. How should sentence 19 be changed?
   Ⓕ Change the word *is* to *were*.
   Ⓖ Change the word *meaning* to did *mean*.
   Ⓗ Move the period inside the quotation marks.
   Ⓙ It should not be changed at all.

Name _____

Using Adjectives in Writing

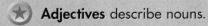

⭐ **Adjectives** describe nouns.

An ecosystem is a community of **living** beings – including plants, animals, and bacteria!

Tall trees, **singing** birds, and **busy** ants are all part of a **forest** ecosystem.

Ⓐ Draw an arrow from the adjective to the noun it describes.

1. Low shrubs and young trees, or underbrush, grow on a forest floor.

2. The underbrush must survive on low light because it is usually shaded by higher branches.

3. Soft, green moss grows on rocks and slow-growing fungus develops on trees.

4. Scaly lizards climb sky-high branches.

5. Silent beetles scuttle under fallen logs to feed.

6. Shy deer with velvety antlers eat bark and green leaves.

7. Playful squirrels hide their precious nuts for later.

8. Bright birds and black snakes make their nests in a hollow tree.

9. Colorful wildflowers bloom where there is enough sunlight.

10. At night, more creatures come out to find leaves and tender branches to eat.

B Complete each sentence with an adjective from the box that fits.

| rural   urban   wild   native   small   large   prairie   many |

1. There are _____ kinds of ecosystems.

2. Some are in _____ areas, while others are in _____ areas.

3. An ecosystem can be as _____ as a puddle or as _____ as an ocean.

4. Both _____ animals and _____ plants live together in an ecosystem.

5. I would love to visit a _____ ecosystem.

C Write two or three sentences to show what you know about using adjectives. Write descriptions of things you might see in a particular ecosystem, or write about another topic of your choice. Use at least one adjective in each sentence.

_____

_____

_____

_____

_____

_____

_____

_____

_____

_____

_____

Name _____

Using Adverbs in Writing

18

ECOSYSTEMS

⭐ **Adverbs** are used to modify verbs, adjectives, and other adverbs. They answer questions such as "how," "how often," "when," "why," "where," and "how much."

Adverbs describe verbs.
   Some coral reefs grow **slowly**.

Adverbs describe adjectives.
   Corals come in **many** different types.

Adverbs describe other adverbs.
   Some corals do grow **quite** quickly.

A **Write near the arrow the kind of word each adverb describes. Use *v* for "verb," *adj* for "adjective," and *adv* for "adverb."**

1. Some people mistakenly think that coral is a plant, but it is an animal.

2. Coral usually live connected in communities.

3. Reefs develop in very shallow water, usually close to shore.

4. A few types of coral aren't hard, but quite soft.

5. Tiny plants called plankton grow very abundantly in reefs.

6. Seaweed also grows protectively around coral.

7. When a sea worm hides in coral, it is not easily found.

8. Some fish swim almost playfully among the coral.

Advantage Grammar Grade 5 © 2005 Creative Teaching Press

B Complete each sentence with an adverb from the box that fits.

| dully   often   slowly   brightly   tightly |

1. Some fish are colored _____ as a warning to others.

2. Other fish want to hide, so they are colored _____.

3. Since reefs are close to the surface, currents and waves _____ affect them.

4. Sea horses have to _____ hold on with their tails to coral to be able to stay in place.

5. Many reefs started growing long ago and are still growing _____.

C Circle the words you find in the word search. Some words are diagonal or spelled in reverse order. List the adverbs.

Y	N	O	W	S	L	S
R	A	F	T	W	O	T
B	R	I	G	H	T	I
C	M	N	F	A	S	L
Y	U	A	G	R	F	L
L	C	L	R	D	A	Y
K	H	L	O	L	S	L
C	Q	Y	W	Y	T	T
I	L	L	T	T	M	E
U	P	G	E	T	A	E
Q	U	I	T	E	N	W
A	T	V	E	R	Y	S
O	S	K	I	P	L	N

Adverbs

_____

_____

_____

_____

_____

_____

_____

_____

_____

_____

_____

Name _____

Word Order in Sentences

⭐ The order of words and phrases in a sentence can change the meaning of the sentence.

Confusing: Lions live in savannas, unlike tigers, not jungles.
(Are savannas unlike tigers?)

Better: Lions, unlike tigers, live in savannas, not jungles.

Keep descriptive words and phrases close to the word being described.

Ⓐ **Put a check next to the sentence that is better.**

1. ___ Sometimes with just a few trees, savannas are tropical grasslands.
   ___ Savannas are tropical grasslands, sometimes with just a few trees.

2. ___ Some streams only appear during the rainy season.
   ___ Only some steams appear during the rainy season.

3. ___ Grasslands to support many trees do not get enough rain.
   ___ Grasslands do not get enough rain to support many trees.

4. ___ Grasses wither in the dry season.
   ___ Grasses in the dry season wither.

5. ___ Zebra and wildebeest migrate to find more grass often.
   ___ Zebra and wildebeest often migrate to find more grass.

6. ___ Giraffes can always stretch up to leaves where no other animals can reach.
   ___ Giraffes can stretch up to leaves always where no other animals can reach.

7. ___ Small bushes also grow in savannas besides the tall grass.
   ___ Besides the tall grass, small bushes also grow in savannas.

8. ___ Most grasslands are not tropical, but prairies in the United States.
   ___ Most grasslands in the United States are not tropical, but prairies.

B Rewrite the sentence to make it better. Move the underlined phrase.

1. Cooler grasslands are called prairies <u>that do not have trees at all</u>.

   _____

2. Most grassland plants <u>so they don't get burned by the sun</u> have thin leaves.

   _____

3. Most of the plant <u>to avoid sun and wind</u> is underground.

   _____

4. American prairies, because so much grain is grown there, <u>are called the Wheat Belt</u>.

   _____

5. Prairie grass is good for grazing animals <u>besides being used for growing food</u>.

   _____

C Use the phrases from the box to write two or three sentences about prairies.

prairie dogs	butterflies	snakes and goldenrod
with color	out of holes	from plant to plant	among the grass

   _____

   _____

   _____

   _____

   _____

   _____

Using Commas in Direct Quotations

20

ECOSYSTEMS

When you use someone's spoken words in a paragraph, use a comma to separate the spoken words from other information about the speaker.

"Hello," said a dark-haired man knocking on the Alaskan sheriff's door.

Keep end punctuation within the quotation marks.

"Tuma and Cloud," said Sheriff Okituk. "You both look upset. Please, won't you come in?"

If a spoken sentence is interrupted by unspoken text, introduce the rest of the sentence with a comma.

"Come in, that is," continued the sheriff, "if you don't mind my child being here."

A **Add commas and quotation marks where they are missing.**

The sheriff nodded then spoke to an unseen person under his desk. "Liak, you can stay if you stay quiet said Sheriff Okituk. Now, what can I do for you gentlemen?

We're having a misunderstanding over a deed, Tuma explained. Cloud held up a piece of paper and said, Oil has just been discovered on my family's land.

Stop right there, said Tuma. It's my family's land, not yours. I could have proved it until my deed was stolen last week.

I know these parts pretty well, and I know who owns what, said the Sheriff. Just tell me where the oil was discovered and I'll know who it belongs to.

But it's not around here said Tuma. It's up north—in the tundra.

Is it even colder up there than it is here? asked a voice from under the desk.

B Add commas and quotation marks where they are missing in the rest of the story.

Quiet, little one, warned Sheriff Okituk.

But Cloud laughed and said, That's right, it's even colder! And you have to be careful the polar bears don't eat you up. Why, my grandfather who owned the land talked about seeing penguins being eaten whole by a bear!

Oh, Daddy said Liak still under the desk now you know who's lying!

Her father laughed and said Yes, even my little girl knows that penguins only live in the *southern* part of the world!

C Add all necessary punctuation to these jokes. Underline any letters that should be capitalized.

1. why did the walrus cross the water asked Baral
   I don't know said Sedna why
   Baral answered to get to the other tide

2. I've got a joke too said Sedna what did the sea say to the iceberg
   you're so cool guessed Baral
   no answered Sedna it didn't say anything. it just waved

3. what is a baby grasshopper after it is six days old asked Sedna
   seven days old said Baral

4. what's a snowy owl's favorite salad asked Baral
   let me guess said Sedna does it have iceberg lettuce

5. here's one more joke about the tundra said Baral What do you call a gigantic polar bear
   nothing said Sedna I wouldn't call it—I would run away

Name _____

Spelling Word Endings

LESSON

21

ECOSYSTEMS

⭐ An **affix** is a word part that can be added to a base word. We add endings to change the tense of a verb, form plurals, make nouns and verbs agree, and make comparisons.

stem—stem**s**   grow—grow**ing**   grow—grow**n**

root—root**ed**   deep—deep**er**   lovely—lovel**iest**

When adding an affix, you sometimes change the spelling of the base word. When adding an affix that begins with a vowel to a base word that ends with silent e, drop the e.

live - liv**ing**

For base words ending with a consonant and y, change the y to i.

pretty — pret**tiest**

For base words ending in a short vowel and a consonant, double the consonant.

swim — swim**ming**

A Write the correct form of the word to complete each sentence.

1. **know** Forests of mangrove trees form what is _____ as the mangroves.

2. **form** Mangroves have always _____ on swampy coastlines.

3. **grow** A root _____ in the air, not in the ground.

4. **find** The root eventually _____ its way into the mud.

5. **build** Then soil starts _____ up around it.

6. **produce** The trees begin _____ a bright red berry.

Advantage Grammar Grade 5 © 2005 Creative Teaching Press

Suffixes are word endings that add meaning to words.

The suffixes *-ion*, *-ence*, and *-ance*, change a verb into a noun. They make the word refer to a "condition" or "action."

assist—assist**ance**

The suffixes *-ful*, *-y*, *-ous*, and *-ious*, mean "having" or "full of." They change a noun into an adjective.

caution—caut**ious**

B **Change the words as directed to complete the puzzle.**

ACROSS

3. Make the verb *educate* a noun.

7. Make the verb *excel* a noun.

9. Make an adjective meaning "full of care."

10. Make the noun *clump* an adjective.

DOWN

1. Make the verb *act* a noun.

2. Make an adjective meaning "having joy."

4. Make the verb *differ* a noun.

5. Make the verb *tense* a noun.

6. Make the verb *appear* a noun.

8. Make the noun *crust* an adjective.

Name _____

Topic and Supporting Sentences

 The **topic sentence** of a paragraph states the main idea. In a paragraph organized around a topic sentence, all the other sentences should support the topic sentence. They should explain more about the topic, or give examples. The topic sentence in the paragraph below is underlined.

Plants and animals depend on each other. Even animals that do not eat plants still need plants. For example, a tree may be an owl's home. A lion may depend on the shade of a tree during the heat of the day. Spider crabs survive, in part, because of the algae camouflage growing on their shells. Plants need animals to scatter their seeds. Another example of a plant needing an animal is when ants eat the coating off a peony's bud, so it can blossom. ~~A peony often has ants on it when cut down.~~

The last sentence is not related to the main idea that plants and animals depend on each other, so it can be left out.

 Read the paragraph. Underline the topic sentence. Cross out the sentence that does not support the topic sentence.

Plants and animals help each other "breathe." Plants use carbon dioxide, sunlight, and water to make food. Plants don't eat like animals do, but they still need energy. As plants make their food, they release oxygen. Animals, including people, breathe in air, use the oxygen, and release the carbon dioxide. This carbon dioxide is then used by plants.

Put a check next to the sentence that would best fit in the paragraph because it supports the topic sentence.

____ Dead plants and animals also give off carbon dioxide, which is then used by plants.

____ Too much carbon dioxide is poisonous for animals.

B **Read the paragraph. Underline the topic sentence. Cross out the sentence that does not support the topic sentence.**

All life needs sunlight. As you know, all plants need sunshine to grow—even plants in the sea. Animals that are active only in the dark still need the sun to grow the plants that they or their prey feed on. Sunlight also warms our earth and the atmosphere to provide a comfortable environment in which life can flourish. It's amazing how something 93 million miles away can make such a difference to life on Earth! The sun is in the center of our solar system.

Place a check next to the sentence that would best fit in the sentence.

_____ Looking directly into the sun can hurt your eyes.

_____ Living things absorb some of the vitamins they need from sunlight.

C **Read the topic sentence. Put an X beside three sentences that you would most likely leave out of a paragraph using the topic sentence because they do NOT support the main idea.**

Topic sentence: All life on Earth needs water.

_____ We can survive weeks without food, but only days without water.

_____ Water tastes so good when you are thirsty!

_____ All plants need water in order to grow.

_____ Some animals and plants can go longer without water than others, but they still need water.

_____ Earth is the only planet in our solar system with liquid water.

_____ About 97% of the water on Earth is salt water.

_____ Most sea creatures die within minutes of being taken out of water.

_____ Pollution hurts everyone.

_____ Believe it or not, some plants will die if they get too much water.

_____ A plants' roots and leaves are designed to collect water.

_____ Camels and cacti store water to use over time.

Name _____

 Editing your work is an important step in the writing process. Many tests ask you to show what you know about editing.

A **Hannah wrote a report on the rain forest. Help her analyze and edit her work. Read the paragraphs and follow the directions.**

Real Rain Forests

1) Many people have learned incorrect facts about the rain forest. 2) Some people call rain forests "jungles." 3) Although some rain forests are jungles, other places can be rain forests, too. 4) The Columbia Encyclopedia says "jungles are a tangled mass of vegetation." 5) Many people wrongly think that rain forests are found only in hot, tropical areas. 6) A few rain forests exist in much cooler areas, such as the state of Oregon. 7) Oregon also has tall, snowy mountains. 8) Rain forests are forests that actually get a lot of rain year round. 9) Some people think that lions and tigers live in rain forests, but only tigers do. 10) Lions live in savannas, where there are few trees.

1. Underline the topic sentence.

2. What word does the adjective *incorrect* describe? _____

3. What needs to be added to sentence 4 and where? _____

4. Which two words are adverbs in sentence 5 and what kinds of words do they describe? _____

5. Rewrite sentence 8 so that it is more clear.

   _____

   _____

6. Cross out the sentence that does not relate to the topic sentence.

Name _____

B **Read Hannah's story about two children from different rain forests. Read the story and help her revise her work.**

World-traveller, Shannon, gave her nephew, Peter, another boy's E-mail address because they both live in rain forests. But they live halfway around the world from each other! Here, the two boys meet online.

1) "Hi," Peter wrote. "My name is Peter. I live near a rain forest in Oregon in the United States."

2) "Hi," Fajar wrote back. "I am Fajar. I live in the rain forest on the island of Borneo in the country of Malaysia."

3) "Wow!" said Peter. "No one here lives right in the rain forest!"

4) "Where else to live is there?" asked Fajar.

5) "We live in towns and cities," said Peter.

6) "We have towns and cities, too," answered Fajar. "But I think more orangutan live in such protected areas than people do."

7) "We don't have orangutans in our forests," wrote Peter. "We see them only at the zoo."

8) "I think only they live on Borneo," wrote Fajar. "But you must have animals there that we don't."

9) "I think it will be fun to find out!" wrote Peter. "I have to go now, but let's do this again."

1. Rewrite line 4 to make it better. _____
_____

2. List the two adjectives in line 6 along with the words they describe.
_____

3. Rewrite line 8 to make it better.
_____
_____

Name _____

Joshua wrote a report on deserts. Help him analyze and edit his work. Read the paragraphs and follow the directions.

Deserts

1) Any area that have less than 10 inches of precipitation is called a desert each year. 2) Precipitation is any form of water falling from the sky, such as rain, hail, or snow. 3) Most deserts are hot and dry, but some deserts are actually cold and dry. 4) Antarctica is a very cold desert. 5) Because both plants and animals need water to live, fewer liveing things exist in deserts. 6) Grass and cactus grown best in deserts. 7) Flowers and even a few trees live in some deserts. 8) We don't go into the desert very much.

1. How should sentence 1 be rewritten?

ⓐ Any area that has less than 10 inches of precipitation each year is called a desert.

ⓑ Each year any area that has less than 10 inches of precipitation is a desert.

ⓒ Any area that has, "less than 10 inches of precipitation" each year is a desert.

ⓓ It does not need to be rewritten.

2. What is true about sentence 4?

ⓕ The word *cold* is an adjective describing *is*.

ⓖ The word *cold* is an adverb describing *is*.

ⓗ The word *very* is an adjective describing *desert*.

ⓙ The word *very* is an adverb describing *cold*.

3. Which sentence does *not* belong in the paragraph?

ⓐ sentence 1   ⓒ sentence 8

ⓑ sentence 4   ⓓ None, all sentences support the main idea.

4. Which incorrect word from the paragraph is paired with its correct spelling?

ⓕ have – haved

ⓖ desert – dessert

ⓗ grown – grows

ⓙ liveing – living

Continue reading and editing Joshua's report.

9) Weather in the desert is interesting. 10) Temperature ranges for just one day may be very wide. 11) Many deserts are too hot during the day and too cold at night. 12) Rainstorms may come—and go—very quickly. 13) Rain often hits only one area. 14) "It seems believable", said one native, "the story of the man who washed his hands in the edge of an Arizona thunder shower without wetting his cuffs." 15) After most desert rains, the water either soaks into the ground or dries up. 16) Many deserts have sunshine and winds daily.

5. Which word from the paragraph is not an adverb?
   Ⓐ too
   Ⓑ just
   Ⓒ wide
   Ⓓ daily

6. Which is true about sentence 14?
   Ⓕ The first comma should be inside the quotation marks.
   Ⓖ The word *wetting* should be spelled *weting*.
   Ⓗ The word *believable* is an adverb describing *seems*.
   Ⓙ The period should come after the last quotation marks.

7. Which word pair is an example of a verb with its related noun?
   Ⓐ quick – quickly
   Ⓑ believe – believable
   Ⓒ winds – windy
   Ⓓ dries – dryness

8. Which statement is true?
   Ⓕ The adverb *very* describes the adjective *quickly*.
   Ⓖ The adverb *very* describes the adverb *quickly*.
   Ⓗ The adverb *very* describes the adverb *wide*.
   Ⓙ The adverb *very* describes the verb *come*.

Name _____

Using Coordinating Conjunctions in Writing

⭐ **Conjunctions** connect words, or groups of words, in a sentence.

Would you rather visit Florida **or** California?

I like to visit Florida for the beaches **and** California for the mountains.

When you use a conjunction to connect more than two items in a series, use **commas** to separate the words.

I have visited Wyoming, Utah, **and** Kansas.

Coordinating Conjunctions	and or nor but

A **Circle the conjunction in each sentence. Add commas where needed in series.**

1. My family and I live in Colorado.

2. The state's name is Spanish for "red" or "ruddy."

3. People enjoy camping hiking and skiing in the Rocky Mountains.

4. Tourists come to see the old mining towns the mountains or the cliff dwellings.

5. Old mining towns are known as ghost abandoned or dead towns.

6. Colorado does not lack industry nor open lands.

7. Farmers and ranchers own half of the land in Colorado.

8. Colorado's region is called the Mountain States the Southwest or simply the West.

B **Write the conjunction to complete each sentence. Add commas where needed.**

1. We flew to the Midwest to see my grandma _____ grandpa.

2. While flying over Kansas, we saw neither mountains _____ deserts.

3. Meeting us at the airport was Grandma _____ not Grandpa.

4. In Missouri, we can travel by car plane train _____ boat.

5. The two major cities in Missouri are St. Louis _____ Kansas City.

Name _____

> ★ Conjunctions can be used to combine sentences
>
> I learned about the Mississippi River. I learned about the states it flows through, too.
>
> I learned about the Mississippi River **and** the states it flows through.

C **Combine the sentences using conjunctions. Remember to use commas when connecting more than two items in a series.**

1. Rivers are used for trade. They are used for travel. Rivers are used for food. Rivers are used for water.

   _____

   _____

2. The Mississippi's waters come from Lake Itasca. The Mississippi's waters come from rivers that flow into it.

   _____

   _____

3. The Missouri River flows into the Mississippi. The Ohio River flows into the Mississippi. The White River flows into the Mississippi. Many other rivers flow into the Mississippi.

   _____

   _____

4. The Colorado River does not flow into the Mississippi. Neither does the Rio Grande flow into the Mississippi.

   _____

   _____

5. People fish for carp in the Mississippi. People fish for perch in the Mississippi. People fish for bass in the Mississippi.

   _____

   _____

Name _____

Using Appositives in Writing

⭐ An **appositive** consists of a word or group of words that comes before or after a noun and renames or identifies it.

The first state to approve the bill, **New Jersey**, celebrates Bill of Rights Day.

An appositive can also further explain a noun.

Inventor **Thomas Edison** lived most of his life in New Jersey.

A Underline the appositive in each sentence.

1. The word Massachusetts was the name of a Native American tribe.

2. New Jersey, the first state to have lifeguards, has a coastline 127 miles long.

3. George Washington became president in the first U.S. capital, New York City.

4. The Appalachian Trail, a 2,100-mile footpath, stretches from Georgia to Maine.

5. Dutch settlers named their colony Rhode Island, or "red island."

6. The "little town too big for one state," Delmar, is partly in Delaware and partly in Maryland.

7. Milk, the official state beverage, is the beverage shared by Vermont, North Carolina, and Virginia.

8. The Hershey chocolate company has made Hershey, Pennsylvania, "the sweetest place on Earth."

9. Many Connecticut towns center around a park, or "green."

10. The first colony to declare independence, New Hampshire, did so six months before the Declaration of Independence was written.

Advantage Grammar Grade 5 © 2005 Creative Teaching Press

B Draw a line from the appositive to the noun it renames, identifies, or explains.

1. Famous soldier Nathan Hale wanted Vermont to be its own country.

2. Georgia, the Peach State, is also known for its peanuts.

3. A Revolutionary War fort, made of spongy Palmetto logs, foiled the British attackers. Their cannonballs bounced right off it.

4. Maine, once part of Massachusetts, produces 99 percent of the blueberries sold in the United States.

5. Presidents Theodore and Franklin Roosevelt made New York their home.

C Write five sentences using appositives. Use the examples in the box or create your own.

my teacher	sports idol	my favorite restaurant
best movie of all time	popular singer	usually done outdoors

_____

_____

_____

_____

_____

_____

_____

_____

_____

_____

Name _____

Writing Complex Sentences

⭐ Some sentences contain an **independent clause**, a phrase that can stand alone because it is a complete sentence, and a **dependent clause**, a sentence fragment.

Although it is rare, it does snow in the Southwest.

dependent clause   *independent clause*

Snow rarely sticks except when it falls in the mountains.

independent clause   *dependent clause*

A Label each phrase with IC for "independent clause" or DC for "dependent clause."

1. Even though they are all on the west coast, California and Washington are

   not considered to be part of the same region.

2. California is in the Southwest, while Washington is part of the Pacific Northwest.

3. While it does not touch any other state, Alaska is generally considered to be

   part of the Pacific Northwest, too.

4. California, Arizona, Nevada, New Mexico, and Texas make up the Southwest

   region because they have similar climates.

5. Because it contains eleven states, the Southeast region is largest.

Name _____

B Add your own independent clause to each dependent clause below to write your own sentences.

Although I hate to admit it,	While I usually enjoy it,
Without seeing the movie yet,	After it was all over,
Because I couldn't do it alone,	During my last visit,

_____

_____

_____

_____

_____

_____

_____

_____

_____

_____

_____

_____

_____

_____

_____

_____

_____

_____

_____

_____

Name _____

Linking Independent Clauses

 When joining two complete sentences that relate, use a comma and a conjunction.

Related:	I thought I had been to all the Midwest states. I have never visited Nebraska.
Joined:	I thought I had been to all the Midwest states, but I have never visited Nebraska.
Related:	I have not seen another country. I do not need to see one.
Joined:	I have not seen another country, nor do I need to see one.

 A **Circle the conjunction joining the sentences. Add a comma in the correct place.**

1. The Great Chicago Fire was quite devastating for only two buildings survived it.

2. In Cleveland, Ohio, you can see the Browns play at Browns Stadium or you can see the Indians play at Jacob's Field.

3. Rathbun Dam is Iowa's largest body of water and Spirit Lake is the largest lake made by a glacier.

4. St. Louis is on the eastern border of Missouri and Kansas City is on the western border.

5. The Ohio River forms the southern border for three states but it flows through only one.

B **Write the conjunction that best completes each sentence.**

1. Kansas City is in Kansas and Missouri, _____ people from both states cheer for Kansas City Royals.

2. Second City, Chicago, was the second largest city in the United States,

_____ it is not anymore.

Advantage Grammar Grade 5 © 2005 Creative Teaching Press

C **If the sentences relate, rewrite the two sentences as one using the conjuctions in the box. Leave pairs of sentences that do not relate as they are.**

and	but	or	nor	for	yet

1. Detroit, Michigan, is called "Motor City." Detroit is also called "Motown."

   _____

2. Dodge City, Kansas, is the windiest city in the United States. Many famous cowboys came from Kansas. _____

   _____

3. Michigan is called the Great Lake State. Michigan does not touch Lake Ontario. _____

   _____

4. The famous monument Mount Rushmore is in South Dakota. North Dakota borders Canada. _____

   _____

5. Ohio is considered part of the Midwest. Ohio is in the easternmost third of the country. _____

   _____

6. We had to drive through Indiana on the way to Illinois. We stopped in Indianapolis to sightsee. _____

   _____

7. We could visit the Mall of America in Minnesota. We could see a Minnesota Twins baseball game. _____

   _____

8. Wisconsin is the dairy capital of the United States. It produces more milk than any other state. _____

   _____

Name _____

Alphabetical Order

⭐ To list words in alphabetical order, compare letters in the same position in each word.

Arkansas comes before *California* because *A* comes before *C*.

Alabama comes before *Alaska* because Alabama's fourth letter, *b*, comes before *Alaska's*, *s*.

A **Circle the state that comes first alphabetically. Underline the letters that you compared in each word.**

1. Connecticut   Delaware   4. Vermont   Virginia

2. Illinois   Idaho   5. Arizona   Arkansas

3. Massachusetts   Maine   6. New Jersey   New York

B **Rewrite each list in alphabetical order.**

1. New York   Florida   Washington

   _____

2. Georgia   Colorado   Hawaii

   _____

3. New Mexico   Rhode Island   Nevada

   _____

4. South Carolina   North Carolina   South Dakota

   _____

5. Oklahoma   Ohio   Oregon

   _____

Advantage Grammar Grade 5 © 2005 Creative Teaching Press

Name _____

C Rewrite the list in alphabetical order.

Kentucky
Florida
Utah
Tennessee
Montana
Texas
Oregon
Michigan
Mississippi
North Dakota

1. _____
2. _____
3. _____
4. _____
5. _____
6. _____
7. _____
8. _____
9. _____
10. _____

D Write the state name that comes first alphabetically in each pair to complete the puzzle. Don't add the space between words in a name like WESTVIRGINIA.

ACROSS

1. Iowa   Ohio
4. Louisiana   Minnesota
7. Missouri   Maryland
9. Montana   Oregon
10. Kansas   Nevada

DOWN

1. Texas   Idaho
2. Arkansas   Alabama
3. Maine   Missouri
5. Vermont   Wyoming
6. Colorado   Connecticut
8. New Jersey New Mexico

Name _____

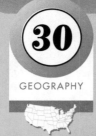

Finding the Topic Sentence

 The topic sentence in a paragraph states the main idea. Usually it appears as the first sentence—but not always. A topic sentence can appear anywhere in a paragraph.

The topic sentence in the following paragraph is the last sentence.

Puerto Rico and Guam are both islands. They are both part of the U.S.A. American Samoa, the Northern Mariana Islands, and the Midway Islands each include three islands apiece in the Pacific Ocean. The Virgin Islands include three islands in the Caribbean Sea, south of Florida. <u>Altogether, the U.S.A. has six territories: Puerto Rico, Guam, American Samoa, the Northern Mariana Islands, the Midway Islands, and the Virgin Islands.</u>

 Underline the topic sentence in each paragraph.

1. The Samoan islands are halfway between Hawaii and New Zealand, in the South Pacific Ocean. The Samoan islands have a tropical climate. In 1899, Germany and the U.S.A. split the islands. The islands once belonging to Germany have since become an independent state, known simply as Samoa. American Samoa, however, still belongs to the U.S.A. Because the islands are so far from other places, the culture of the Samoans has changed little over the years. Samoa certainly has an interesting and unique history.

2. If you are a history buff, you may already know about the Midway Islands. The Midway Islands are a territory of the U.S.A. There are three islands that make up the territory. No people lived on the islands until the U.S.A. claimed them as their own. Because it is in the middle of the Pacific Ocean, Midway was used as a stop to refuel for planes and boats. This was especially important during war times. Now the three islands are a national wildlife refuge.

 Advantage Grammar Grade 5 © 2005 Creative Teaching Press

Name _____

 Once in a while, the main idea is not stated in a topic sentence. The main idea may be split between sentences. Or, the ideas may be obvious.

The main idea of the paragraph below is that Puerto Rico is the United States' closest territory.

Puerto Rico an island is south of Florida in the Caribbean Sea, which is part of the Atlantic Ocean. Puerto Rico, meaning "rich port," has a tropical climate. Although many people know English, the primary language is Spanish. Given the option to become a state, Puerto Rico voted to continue being a territory. Still, many people believe that Puerto Rico will become the fifty-first state.

B **Determine the main idea of the paragraph, then write a topic sentence for it.**

1. There are 100 islands that make up the Virgin Islands. Of these, 68 belong to the United States. Only three of these are even listed on a map: St. Thomas, St. John, and St. Croix. Most of the other islands have no people living on them. Also, St. John is almost completely covered by a national park. Some food crops are raised on the islands, but the biggest business is tourism.

_____

_____

_____

2. The territories are all small islands. While they don't have all the same rights, people in the territories are United States citizens. Just like each state, each territory has a governor. The United States government protects the territories. The territories use the same money used in the United States. The territories are sometimes given the option of becoming a state.

_____

_____

_____

Name _____

31

GEOGRAPHY

Editing Your Work

 Editing your work is an important step in the writing process. Many tests ask you to show what you know about editing.

A **Brian wrote a report about living in Hawaii. Help him analyze and edit the first two paragraphs. Read Brian's report and follow the directions.**

Living in Hawaii

1) When I was little, my family lived in Hawaii. 2) We lived on a beautiful island, Oahu. 3) We moved there for Dad's job. 4) He works for the Navy although he is not in the military. 5) That is called a civilian. 6) My family lived in the capital city, Honolulu.

7) Along with Oahu, there are seven other main islands, as well: Hawaii, Maui, Niihau, Lanai, Kauai, Molokai, and Kahoolawe. 8) You have probably heard of the islands of Hawaii and Maui. 9) Altogether, Hawaii actually has over 130 islands. 10) But not every one has people living on it. 11) All the Hawaiian islands were formed by volcanoes. 12) In fact, there are four active volcanoes even today! 13) The volcanoes don't erupt in violent explosions. 14) The hot lava is still dangerous.

1. Write the independent clause from sentence 1.

_____

2. List the two appositives from the first paragraph (sentences 1–6).

_____

3. Write the list of the major Hawaiian islands in alphabetical order.
Oahu, Hawaii, Maui, Niihau, Lanai, Kauai, Molokai, Kahoolawe

_____

_____

4. Combine sentences 13 and 14 into one sentence.

_____

Advantage Grammar Grade 5 © 2005 Creative Teaching Press

B **Continue reading and editing Brian's report on Living in Hawaii.**

15) Hawaii is the youngest state. 16) It became a state less than fifty years ago! 17) That means that it was still a territory when Pearl Harbor was bombed.

18) Hawaii is so far from the rest of the United States, it isn't even on some U.S.A. maps. 19) It takes a long time to get to Hawaii. 20) From the closest airport, Los Angeles Airport, it takes almost six hours. 21) Since we were moving from Boston, Massachusetts, we first had to fly across the country. 22) We changed planes in Chicago, so it took 15 hours to go from Boston to Hawaii!

23) But once we were there, it was worth it. 24) Hawaii has a tropical climate. 25) This means that it is always warm. 26) Even in the winter, it never got colder than 50°. 27) We could swim almost year-round. 28) Being on islands, Hawaiians seem to live at the ocean. 29) People in Hawaii like to swim, surf, snorkel, and boat.

1. Combine two sentences from the first paragraph into one sentence.

_____

_____

_____

2. What is the appositive in sentence 20 and what does it rename or explain?

_____

3. Find the sentence in the last paragraph that is missing a comma. Add the comma and circle it.

4. Write the words from sentence 25 in alphabetical order.

_____

_____

_____

5. Which sentence is the topic sentence for the first paragraph? _____

Name _____

Take a Test Drive

Fill in the bubble beside the correct answer.

Olivia wrote an essay about foods in different U.S. regions. Help her analyze and edit her essay. Read the first part of Olivia's essay and answer the questions. Circle the letter of the correct answer.

1) In general, many favorite foods are very different across the United States. 2) Part of this is because people in different regions came from various parts of the world. 3) For example, Southwesterners eat more burritos because more of the people came from Mexico. 4) Where burritos were invented. 5) Also, real bagels are found mostly in places with many Jewish people, like New England.

1. In sentence 3, what part of the sentence is *because more of their people came from Mexico*?
   Ⓐ dependent clause   Ⓒ conjunction
   Ⓑ independent clause Ⓓ appositive

2. What is the best way to combine sentences 3 and 4?
   Ⓕ For example, Southwesterners eat more burritos because more of the people came from Mexico, where burritos were invented.
   Ⓖ For example, Southwesterners eat more burritos because more of the people came from Mexico, and where burritos were invented.
   Ⓗ For example, Southwesterners eat more burritos because more of the people came from Mexico and Where burritos were invented.
   Ⓙ Sentences 3 and 4 are not related, so they should not be combined.

3. In sentence 5, what part of the sentence is *like New England*?
   Ⓐ dependent clause   Ⓒ conjunction
   Ⓑ independent clause Ⓓ appositive

4. Which sentence is the topic sentence?
   Ⓕ sentence 1   Ⓗ sentence 4
   Ⓖ sentence 2   Ⓙ sentence 5

Name _____

Read the rest of Olivia's essay and answer the questions. Circle the letter of the correct answer.

6) People also choose their menu from what is most available in their area. 7) For example, people on the coasts eat lots more seafood. 8) Midwestern states grow and eat many grains. 9) The Midwest is often called "the breadbasket."

10) Chain restaurants, like McDonalds, The Olive Garden and Dunkin Donuts, are making it so that more people across the country eat the same things. 11) But even these restaurants sometimes have different items on the menu. 12) For example, McDonalds in Hawaii serves rice. 13) One thing is for sure: whatever food it is, Americans love to eat!

5. Add "like wheat," to sentence 8 after "many grains." What part of the sentence would it be?
   Ⓐ an independent clause
   Ⓑ a dependent clause
   Ⓒ a conjunction
   Ⓓ an appositive

6. What is the best way to combine sentences 8 and 9?
   Ⓕ Midwestern states grow and eat many grains, the Midwest is often called "the breadbasket."
   Ⓖ Midwestern states grow and eat many grains, and the Midwest is often called "the breadbasket."
   Ⓗ Midwestern states grow and eat many grains, so the Midwest is often called "the breadbasket."
   Ⓙ Midwestern states grow and eat many grains, but the Midwest is often called "the breadbasket."

7. What change, if any, should be made to sentence 10?
   Ⓐ Add a comma after "The Olive Garden."
   Ⓑ Add the conjunction *and* after "Dunkin Donuts."
   Ⓒ Change the order of the restaurants to "Dunkin Donuts, The Olive Garden, and McDonalds."
   Ⓓ Do not change the sentence.

8. Which list is in alphabetical order?
   Ⓕ grains, grits, grapes   Ⓗ seafood, salmon, seal
   Ⓖ favorite, foods, for   Ⓙ popcorn, pizza, pancakes

Name _____

33

BOOKS AND
LITERATURE

Using Prepositional Phrases in Writing

 A **prepositional phrase** is used in writing to show how things are related.

on a table   under a table   with a table
near a table   against a table

Prepositional phrases also give time and place information, or tell a condition in which something happens.

during the movie   except for me   without the frosting

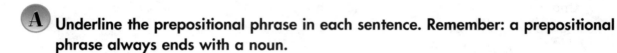

A **Underline the prepositional phrase in each sentence. Remember: a prepositional phrase always ends with a noun.**

1. I wrote the date on my calendar.

2. The vase in the cupboard is my favorite.

3. We'll go after school.

4. We went to the library.

5. The shoes with pockets are the ones I want.

6. Try the cookies in the box.

7. My friend lives down the street.

8. My dog stops at each corner.

9. My room is a mess according to my mom.

10. Throughout the day, I felt so tired.

11. He threw the ball toward the yard.

12. Until today, I have always wanted to go there.

Name _____

 A **preposition** starts each prepositional phrase and a noun ends it.
Below are some examples of prepositions.

about	above	across	after	around	at	before	behind
below	beside	between	by	during	except	for	from
in	into	near	of	over	through	to	toward	under
until	with	without	because of	instead of	out of		

 Underline the four prepositional phrases in the poem below.

Rainy Day

Rainy day, rainy day, I like it;
My mother will come here with my umbrella,
Pitch pitch, chap chap, run run run!

Bag on my shoulder, I follow my mother;
A bell is ringing somewhere,
Pitch pitch, chap chap, run run run!

Oh oh, that girl is dripping wet;
She is crying under the willow,
Pitch pitch, chap chap, run run run!

Mother, mother, I'll lend my umbrella;
"Hi girl, use this umbrella,"
Pitch pitch, chap chap, run run run!

I am all right, don't worry,
Mother will take me in her big umbrella,
Pitch pitch, chap chap, run run run!

Translated from the Japanese by Ayako Egawa

C **Write your own prepositional phrase to answer the question and complete each sentence.**

1. My mother will come here (when?) _____

2. My mother will come here (how?) _____

3. I carry a bag (where?) _____

4. That girl is crying (where?) _____

5. That girl is crying (how) _____

6. Mother will take me (where?) _____

7. Mother will take me (when?) _____

8. Mother will take me (how?) _____

Using Comparatives and Superlatives in Writing

★ When writing about how two or more things compare with one another, add the endings *-er* or *-est* if the word is short.

The Tinman seemed **smarter** than the Cowardly Lion.
The Scarecrow seemed **smartest** of all the friends.

For longer words, add the words *more* or *most*.

I think the Scarecrow is **more interesting** than the Tinman.
Dorothy is the **most interesting** character in the book.

Use *-er* or *more* when comparing two things.

The Wicked Witch of the West was **meaner** than her sister.

Use *-est* or *most* when comparing more than two.

The Wicked Witch was the **meanest** person in the story.

A **Complete each sentence with the correct word or words.**

1. (lonely) Dorothy felt _____ when she first went to Oz.

2. (short) A Munchkin is _____ than a child.

3. (ugly) Of all the people in Oz, the Witch was the _____ .

4. (fast) The Scarecrow was fast, but Toto was the _____ of the group.

5. (bright) The Yellow Brick Road was the _____ in the land.

6. (sleepy) The poppies made Dorothy _____ than the rest.

7. (old) The dark forest seemed _____ than the apple orchard.

8. (scary) Was the Witch or the Winged Monkeys _____ ?

9. (smart) The Scarecrow was _____ than he thought!

10. (afraid) The Wizard was _____ than the Cowardly Lion.

11. (long) Of the book, the play, and the movie, the book is the _____ .

Name _____

 Read the sentence and find the mistake.

If he had had one, the Woodman's heart would have been more loud.

The mistake is in the use of the words *more loud*. Since loud is a short word, simply add *-er* to form the comparative.

If he had had one, the Woodman's heart would have been louder.

B **Cross out the mistake in each sentence. Write the correct word or words, then give a reason for the change.**

1. When the Tinman entered the great Throne Room he saw neither the Head nor the Lady, for Oz had taken the shape of a more terrible Beast.

   _____

   _____

2. The Beast had a head like that of a rhinoceros, only there were a greatest

   number of eyes in its face. _____

   _____

3. It was most big than an elephant, and the green throne seemed hardly strong

   enough to hold its weight. _____

   _____

4. Thick, woolly hair covered every part of it, and a dreadfuler monster could not

   be imagined. _____

   _____

5. But the Tinman was most disappointed than he was afraid.

   _____

   _____

Name _____

Using Transitions in Writing

 Transitions in writing help connect ideas. For example:

> The Mississippi is well worth reading about. It is not a commonplace river. It is in all ways remarkable.

Better:

> The Mississippi is well worth reading about. It is not a commonplace river, **but on the contrary**, it is in all ways remarkable.

Transitions show such ideas as time sequence, comparisons, and causes.

> It seems safe to say that it is **also** the crookedest river in the world, **since** in one part of its journey it uses up one thousand three hundred miles to cover the same ground that the crow would fly over in six hundred and seventy-five.

 A **Here are more sentences from Mark Twain's, *Life on the Mississippi*. Read them and underline words and phrases that connect ideas. There are at least six transitions below.**

From the junction of the Ohio to a point halfway down to the sea, the width averages a mile in high water. From there to the sea the width steadily diminishes, until, at the "Passes," above the mouth, it is but little over half a mile.

The Mississippi's mud builds land fast enough in protected regions higher up. For instance, Prophet's Island contained one thousand five hundred acres of land thirty years ago. Since then, the river has added seven hundred acres to it.

B Write the letter of the best transition to use in the sentence.

____ 1. _____ Mark Twain worked on a boat on the Mississippi River.

____ 2. _____ Twain got his pen name from working on the boat.

____ 3. _____ his name is Samuel Clemens.

____ 4. _____ Twain also gave talks and wrote for newspapers and magazines.

____ 5. _____ Mark Twain had many different experiences.

A. Actually,

B. All in all,

C. Before he wrote books,

D. Besides writing books,

E. In fact,

C Write your own paragraph using transitions to connect ideas. You do not need a transition in every sentence. Use the transitions below or others you know.

for example	then	first	also	of course	finally
therefore	meanwhile	because	afterward		

_____

_____

_____

_____

_____

_____

_____

_____

_____

_____

Name _____

Commonly Misspelled Words

 Words that sound or look alike are often misused.

Use the following rules:

passed/past—*Passed* means "to move by something," *past* means "an earlier time."

except/accept—*Except* means "to leave out," *accept* means "to receive."

no/know/now—*No* means "not," *know* means "to understand," *now* means "the current time"

loose/lose—*Loose* means "not contained" or "baggy," *lose* means "to mislay"

quite/quiet—*quite* means "very," *quiet* means "soft" or "silent"

sense/since—*sense* means a feeling, *since* means "after" or "because of"

who's/whose—*who's* means "who is," *whose* shows ownership

were/where—*were* means "used to be," *where* indicates a place

---

 A **Circle the correct word.**

1. I put my watch in my pocket so I wouldn't (loose/lose) it.

2. The dog seemed lonely (sense/since) the kids returned to school.

3. Did you notice (who's/whose) sweatshirt this is?

4. The bees (were/where) flying among the flowers.

5. A library is known to be a very (quite/quiet) place.

6. In the (passed/past), I went to bed earlier.

7. I do not (no/know/now) how to cook much yet.

8. Everyone went to sleep right away (except/ accept) for me.

9. Put the book on my desk (sense/since) that's where it was before.

10. Grandpa often jingles the (loose/lose) change in his pocket.

11. The fast rabbit (passed/past) the turtle quickly.

12. It is better to finish your work (no/know/now) rather than later.

13. This is a picture of Nana, (who's/whose) my favorite grandparent.

14. We were (quite/quiet) happy when we heard the good news.

B Complete the fairy tale about the dog, Old Sultan, by writing the correct word in each blank.

A shepherd had a faithful dog _____ name was Sultan. One day the shepherd said to his wife, "Sultan is too old to help me _____ . Tomorrow I must get rid of him."

The shepherd's wife said, "I don't want to _____ him, he has been a good dog to us."

"Yes," said the shepherd, "he has been _____ good, but his time of usefulness has _____ ."

Sultan was very _____ when he heard his owners talking about him. He also did not want to _____ the fact that he would have to go away.

Sultan went to talk to his friend the wolf. "Hello, Wolf," said Sultan. "I don't _____ what to do. Can you help me?" Sultan explained what the shepherd had said.

" _____ you have been such a good friend to me, I will help you," said Wolf. "Go with the family when they take a walk tonight. You will _____ me nearby and you will know what to do."

Later, Sultan did go with the family on a walk. When the shepherd set his baby down, Wolf ran out. He grabbed the child's _____ clothing and carried him away. Sultan ran after his friend barking _____ angrily. Wolf dropped the baby _____ the shepherd's wife could pick him up.

" _____ going to get rid of Sultan now?" asked the shepherd's wife petting the old dog.

"Not me!" said the shepherd. "Sultan will have the same life he had with us before _____ he won't have to work anymore." Sultan's days _____ comfortably and they all lived happily ever after.

Name _____

37

BOOKS AND
LITERATURE

Combining Sentences

⭐ Sentences with common elements can sound choppy, especially when they are short.

The Emperor of the small country was proud. The Emperor was also very vain.

Combine these sentences to smooth out the flow.

The Emperor of the small country was proud and very vain.

A Combine the sentences.

1. The Emperor loved to show off. Most of all, he loved to dress up.

   _____

2. Two fortune-hunters passed through the country. They heard about the Emperor's wealth. They also heard about his vanity.

   _____

   _____

3. The two men sneaked around the palace. They stole fancy clothes right off the drying line! Then they dressed in the fanciest clothes.

   _____

   _____

4. The servants noticed the fancy clothes. They knew their ruler would be interested in buying more. They brought the "tailors" to see him.

   _____

   _____

5. The "tailors" bragged about their clothes. They said they had a special property. They said that anyone who did not deserve his position would not be able to see the clothes.

   _____

   _____

Advantage Grammar Grade 5 © 2005 Creative Teaching Press

Name _____

B **Rewrite the ending of Hans Christian Anderson's story "The Emperor's New Clothes" combining sentences to make it flow better.**

The "tailors" brought the final work to him. The Emperor could not see anything. But he did not want anyone to think he was unfit to be ruler. The Emperor said that he loved the new clothes. The lords and ladies also did not want to look bad. They said that they loved the clothes, too.

One "tailor" said that the Emperor should have a royal parade for all to see. The Emperor liked the idea of showing off. He decided to have the parade. The "tailors" took their payment. They left the land before the parade.

The Emperor started his parade. But no one could see his new clothes. Everyone was afraid. So all his subjects shouted praises. They clapped for the new clothes. One little boy did not understand what was happening. He could not see the clothes. He thought the Emperor looked silly. The little boy shouted, "Look! The Emperor has no clothes!" Then the Emperor knew that he had been tricked. He was very embarrassed. He tried to find the "tailors" to punish them. The "tailors" were already gone.

_____

_____

_____

_____

_____

_____

_____

_____

_____

_____

_____

_____

_____

Name _____

Punctuating Titles

 Titles of long works are put in italics or underlined. These include the titles of novels, movies, albums, newspapers, magazines, ships, and planes.

My favorite book is *The Phantom Tollbooth* by Norton Juster. Another great book is <u>West African Folk Tales</u>.

Titles of shorter works are put in quotation marks. These works include titles of songs, chapters, articles, short poems, and short stories. As in writing dialogue, quotation marks go outside commas and periods.

One funny story is "The Cow-Tail Switch."

A **Add underlines or quotation marks. Some sentences may have more than one title in it!**

1. The babysitter read the children the book, Biscuit.

2. The children's parents told the story, Chicken Little.

3. We sailed the bay in the boat, The Apple Pie.

4. People read the forecast in our newspaper, The Times Journal.

5. My name was mentioned in the article, Locals Win Awards.

6. The plane marked RX395 is nicknamed Romeo for short.

7. We sang Rain, Rain, Go Away all day long.

8. Many people like the song, Circle of Life from the movie, The Lion King.

9. The funniest section in the magazine Reader's Digest is called Humor in Uniform.

10. Aesop's Fables includes the story, The Tortoise and the Hare.

11. My favorite song from the movie, Snow White is Heigh-Ho.

12. Yesterday we read the chapter, Bad News in the book, Charlotte's Web.

B List titles for each.

1. two of your favorite books: _____

    _____

2. a chapter in a book: _____

3. two of your favorite songs: _____

    _____

4. the title of a CD: _____

5. the name of a ship: _____

6. the name of a newspaper: _____

7. the names of two magazines: _____

    _____

8. the title of a magazine or newspaper article: _____

9. the name of your favorite movie: _____

    _____

10. the name of a short story or poem: _____

C Write a few sentences about your favorite book or CD. Give the title and a short description. Then tell your favorite chapter or song and tell why it is your favorite.

_____

_____

_____

_____

_____

_____

_____

Name _____

Editing Your Work

 Editing your work is an important step in the writing process. Many tests ask you to show what you know about editing.

A **Christopher wrote a book report about his favorite book. Help him analyze and edit his report. Read the report and answer the questions that follow.**

The Trumpet of the Swan

1) I recently reread my favorite book, The Trumpet of the Swan, by E. B. White. 2) E. B. White also wrote the popular book Charlotte's Web. 3) We read Charlotte's Web a few years ago in school. 4) But I think The Trumpet of the Swan is most interesting. 5) That is because it seems real.

6) The book is about a swan named Louis. 7) Louis is normal accept for one thing—he is mute. 8) That means he cannot make a sound, but is always quite. 9) Louis's father steals a trumpet for him. 10) Then Louis travels the country on an adventure as he learns to play the trumpet.

11) My favorite chapter is called Boston. 12) In that chapter, Louis gets a job playing music on a famous boat, The Swan. 13) Now I would like to visit the city of Boston and the park where the real swan boats are.

1. Add quotation marks or underlines to the six titles in the report.

2. Choose two sentences that can be combined. Rewrite them as one here.

_____

_____

_____

3. Write the incorrect word used in sentence 4 and write the word that should be used in its place.

_____

4. Write the two incorrect words in the second paragraph. Then write the words that should have been used.

_____

 Advantage Grammar Grade 5 © 2005 Creative Teaching Press

Name _____

 B **Read what Christopher wrote about the movie version of his favorite book. Help him revise and edit his report. Read the report and answer the questions that follow.**

The Trumpet of the Swan—The Movie

14) My mom new that The Trumpet of the Swan is my favorite book. 15) So she bought me the movie for Christmas. 16) I'm not going to tell her, but I really hate it. 17) It does not follow the plot of the book very well.

18) It seems like it was written for little kids. 19) For one thing, they left out all the sad parts. 20) Also the songs are stupid. 21) The songs were boring, too. 22) But I admit, one song, Louie, Louie, Louie, was fun.

23) The only part of the movie that I liked was Louis's father. 24) He was even hilariouser in the movie than in the book. 25) But I did not like the animation showing all the places were Louis went. 26) They did not look at all like how I pictured them from the book. 27) So, I think anyone should skip the movie and just read the book! 28) The Trumpet of the Swan is one movie that is just going to stay on the shelf.

1. Add quotation marks and underlines to the titles in the report.

2. Write the incorrect word from the first paragraph and write the word that should be used. _____

3. List the two transitional phrases from the second paragraph.

   _____

4. Combine two sentences from the second paragraph. Rewrite them here as one.

   _____

   _____

5. Write the two incorrect words in the third paragraph. Then write the words that should have been used.

   _____

6. List at least two prepositional phrases from the report.

   _____

   _____

   _____

Name _____

LESSON

40

BOOKS AND
LITERATURE

Take a Test Drive

Fill in the bubble beside the correct answer.

Sarah wrote a report comparing a book and its movies. Help her analyze and edit her report. Read the report and answer the questions that follow.

Freaky Friday—the Book and the Movies

1) Ever sense I saw the movie <u>Freaky Friday</u> I wanted to read the book. 2) Then I found out that there was also another movie. 3) It was out when my mom was my age. 4) So I studied all three versions. 5) It was good I did, because all three versions were so different from each other.

6) The book and the first movie have little in common—accept for the fact that Mary Rodgers wrote both of them! 7) The book was more calm than the movie. 8) But it did have some crazy parts. 9) Still, there was no water-skiing through the boss's tent in the book. 10) But the book and the movie had the same characters and the same beginning.

1. Which statement is true about sentence 1?
   - Ⓐ It should be combined with sentence 2.
   - Ⓑ The movie title should be in quotation marks, not underlined.
   - Ⓒ The word *sense* should be replaced with the word *since*.
   - Ⓓ Nothing should be changed, it is perfect.

2. Which two sentences in the first paragraph should be combined?
   - Ⓕ sentences 1 and 2   Ⓗ sentences 3 and 4
   - Ⓖ sentences 2 and 3   Ⓙ sentences 4 and 5

3. Which word from the first paragraph is NOT a transition?
   - Ⓐ Then   Ⓒ It
   - Ⓑ So   Ⓓ because

4. What is true about the word *accept* in sentence 6?
   - Ⓕ It should be replaced with the word *except*.
   - Ⓖ It is part of a transition.
   - Ⓗ It should be replaced with the word *acceptest*.
   - Ⓙ It is part of a prepositional phrase.

Advantage Grammar Grade 5 © 2005 Creative Teaching Press

Name _____

Read the rest of Sarah's report and answer the questions.

11) The new movie and the old movie are even differenter. 12) In the old movie, the girl is named Annabel. 13) In the old movie, the mom is Ellen. 14) In the new movie, the girl is Anna and the mom is Tess. 15) Another difference is that Ellen is still married to Annabel's dad, while Tess is divorced and about to get married to someone knew. 16) Annabel and Ellen switch because it is Friday the Thirteenth. 17) Anna and Tess switch because of an ancient Chinese curse.

18) The music is also different. 19) The old movie has know interesting music. 20) But Anna, whose in a band, plays cool music. 21) I especially like the song from the new movie What I Like About You. 22) The only thing that's the same in the new movie and the old is the main idea—a mother and daughter don't get along, but switching places changes their minds about each other.

5. What word or phrase should replace *differenter*?
    Ⓐ differentest   Ⓒ most different
    Ⓑ more different   Ⓓ Don't change it, it is correct.

6. Which two sentences could be combined?
    Ⓕ sentences 12 and 13   Ⓗ sentences 18 and 19
    Ⓖ sentences 15 and 16   Ⓙ sentences 21 and 22

7. Which change is NOT correct?
    Ⓐ sentence 15—*knew* should be *new*
    Ⓑ sentence 19—*know* should be *no*
    Ⓒ sentence 20—*whose* should be *who's*
    Ⓓ sentence 22—*new* should be *knew*

8. Which is the best correction for a title?
    Ⓕ Friday the Thirteenth should be in quotation marks
    Ⓖ Friday the Thirteenth should be underlined or in italics
    Ⓗ What I Like About You should be in quotation marks
    Ⓙ What I Like About You should be underlined or in italics

9. Which is a prepositional phrase?
    Ⓐ about to get
    Ⓑ because it is
    Ⓒ is also different
    Ⓓ in a band

Name _____

JUST FOR FUN

Independent and Dependent Clauses

⭐ An **independent clause** has a subject and a predicate. It can stand alone as a complete sentence and still make sense.

> My family members are big sports fans, but we all like different games.

> My family members are big sports fans. But we all like different games.

A **dependent clause** may have a subject and a predicate, but it cannot stand alone because it is not a complete sentence.

> After the team practiced for several weeks.
> Who are big fans of the sport.
> What the coach will do after the tournaments.

A Label each clause with *IC* for "independent clause" or *DC* for "dependent clause."

____ **1.** I like the game of ice hockey.

____ **2.** Who is in the penalty box.

____ **3.** Before the match even started.

____ **4.** The goalie is my favorite player.

____ **5.** What he did before he played the game.

____ **6.** Anyone who watches a match.

____ **7.** The puck flew into the goal.

____ **8.** All players are great skaters.

____ **9.** Although it may look dangerous.

____ **10.** Because my team hasn't won this year.

____ **11.** The term *hat trick* comes from hockey.

____ **12.** When a player scores three goals in a game.

Advantage Grammar Grade 5 © 2005 Creative Teaching Press

B **Label each clause with *IC* for "independent clause" or *DC* for "dependent clause."**

1. Every baseball team wears dark uniforms   when playing at home.
        _____   _____

2. Whomever the team played   they tried to be nice to their opponents.
        _____   _____

3. The players threw the ball   from one side of the field to the other.
        _____   _____

4. Mom sat next to Mrs. Murphy   who has a daughter on the other team.
        _____   _____

5. By the time the game started,   all the players were warmed up.
        _____   _____

6. The scores were always tied,   which made for an exciting game.
        _____   _____

7. As the runner neared home,   her teammates all stood to watch and cheer.
        _____   _____

8. The trouble was   that the other team hadn't practiced enough.
        _____   _____

9. Whichever team won the game,   that team would go on to the tournaments.
        _____   _____

10. The tournaments would be at Forrest Field,   which was in our hometown.
         _____   _____

C **A comma sometimes separates a dependent clause from an independent clause. Write a sentence or two telling what other clues helped you decide if a clause was dependent or independent.**

_____

_____

_____

_____

_____

_____

Name _____

Independent and Dependent Clauses

⭐ Remember, an **independent clause** has a subject and a predicate.
A **dependent clause** cannot stand alone.

By the time we arrived at the beach, there was a huge crowd already.

dependent clause   *independent clause*

A **Use the clues you learned from the previous lesson to find, underline, and label each dependent and independent clause.**

1. Finally we could see why there was such a fuss.

2. Standing in the middle of the crowd, there was a volleyball net.

3. Although most teams have more players, each side had only three players each.

4. I recognized one player, who was my neighbor.

5. The players were sweating even though it was cool on the beach.

6. Since there were so few players, each person got to play a lot.

7. We loved watching how the players spiked the ball over the net.

8. After watching the match, we all wanted to play, too!

Advantage Grammar Grade 5 © 2005 Creative Teaching Press

Name _____

 Some dependent clauses appear in the middle of a sentence.

> The center, <u>who is in my math class</u>, can shoot really well.
> *dependent clause*

Both parts of *The center* and *can shoot really well* make up one complete independent clause.

Some sentences do not have any dependent clauses.

> <u>The fan in the stands caught the ball</u>, <u>and he would not throw it back in the game.</u>
> *independent clause*   *independent clause*

In some sentences, the dependent clause makes up the subject or completes the predicate.

> <u>What I would like to do on vacation</u> is play beach volleyball.
> *dependent clause as the subject*

> The nice thing about playing on the beach is <u>that the ground is soft</u>.
> *dependent clause as the predicate*

B **Underline each dependent clause. Write the number of independent clauses in each sentence. Not every sentence will have a dependent clause.**

_____ **1.** We sat in the stands, but actually we usually stood to cheer!

_____ **2.** After we watched the game, my friends and I played three-on-three.

_____ **3.** It was a lot of ground that each player had to cover!

_____ **4.** My friends wanted to see what was going on at the park.

_____ **5.** My sister, who is very fast, also came to play.

_____ **6.** Mom called to see when we'd be home.

_____ **7.** Some of us think that we could play professionally.

_____ **8.** Many athletes go straight into a major-league team after graduation, but others become professional by first playing for a minor-league team.

Name _____

Forming Negative Sentences

 To make a sentence negative, add *not* between the helping verb and the verb.

> I **will** visit you tonight.
> I **will not** visit you tonight.

To make a past-tense sentence negative, add *did not* before the verb and change the verb to its basic form.

> We **played** computer games yesterday.
> We **did not play** computer games yesterday.

If the verb is a form of *to*, simply add *not* after the verb.

> We **were** bored with our new games
> We **were not** bored with our new games.

A **Rewrite each sentence to create a negative sentence.**

1. We like online gaming.

   _____

2. My brother plays against other people.

   _____

3. He is good at some games.

   _____

4. I would rather play a game in person.

   _____

5. I practice on my own before I go online.

   _____

6. It is fun to talk with my friends online.

   _____

7. Last night I talked to my grandma online.

   _____

8. I think the phone is better than the computer.

   _____

 Advantage Grammar Grade 5 © 2005 Creative Teaching Press

Name _____

⭐ When writing a negative sentence, use only one negative word.

Incorrect:

I **don't** have **no** website of my own.   I **never** had **no** website of my own.

Correct:

I have **no** website of my own yet.   I **never** had a website of my own.

The only negative words you can use together are **neither** and **nor**.

My little sister has **neither** a website **nor** an email address.

B Find and circle words in the word search that can be used as negatives. Look up, down, and diagonally for these ten words: *no, not, never, neither, nor, cannot, barely, unable, none,* and *hardly*

```
R  N  Y  O  T  L  X  R  M  I
E  D  B  A  R  E  L  Y  L  O
V  E  C  R  E  F  P  H  E  R
E  P  A  E  H  A  R  D  L  Y
N  O  N  O  T  I  C  C  A  S
A  I  N  N  I  U  R  O  I  N
Z  R  O  P  E  O  L  U  R  G
R  N  T  U  N  A  B  L  E  J
E  Y  S  L  O  R  N  T  G  P
```

C Write two of your own negative sentences using words you found in the word search above.

_____

_____

_____

_____

Name _____

Spelling Contractions

⭐ Contractions join two words together. They are often used in informal speech and writing. The apostrophe (') takes the place of the letters that have been left out.

she had = she'd	you are = you're	it is = it's	it has = it's
I am = I'm	would have = would've	let us = let's	he will = he'll

A few contractions are irregular.

will not = won't   cannot = can't   do not = don't

A Circle the contraction. Write the words that formed the contraction.

1. I won't be going online tonight. _____

2. I didn't use the computer last night either. _____

3. If I had, I would've gotten your message sooner. _____

4. My brother said he'd be on the computer all evening. _____

5. He's trying to catch up on his homework. _____

6. Please tell me when you'll be online again. _____

7. We're going to have to use a new instant messaging program. _____

8. My dad couldn't fix the bugs in the last program. _____

9. It seems like there's always a new virus going around. _____

10. We can't stand the thought of a virus hurting our system. _____

11. It's a shame when that happens to a computer. _____

12. I'll let you know when we can meet online again! _____

Advantage Grammar Grade 5 © 2005 Creative Teaching Press

Name _____

B Complete the sentence with the correct contraction.

1. My teacher (was not) _____ going to post our homework online.

2. Then he learned that (we would) _____ use it.

3. He said (he would) _____ start our own class website.

4. Now (it has) _____ taken on a life of its own!

5. We (cannot) _____ find enough time to visit the site.

6. We promise that we (will not) _____ forget to check the calendar.

7. Our teacher (has not) _____ forgotten to update our site.

8. I (will not) _____ forget to send you the link to the site.

9. (Let us) _____ give each other our E-mail addresses.

10. I hope (you will) _____ check the site, too.

C Write three or four of your own sentences using contractions.

_____

_____

_____

_____

_____

_____

_____

_____

Advantage Grammar Grade 5 © 2005 Creative Teaching Press   91

Name _____

Using Apostrophes

⭐ In addition to spelling a contraction, an apostrophe can also be used to show **possession**, or ownership.

  a boy's bike = the bike belonging a boy
  Nikki's dog = the dog belonging to Nikki

Apostrophes are NOT used with possessive pronouns.

  her dog = the dog belonging to her
  its leash = the leash belonging to it

A **Circle *P* for "possessive" or *C* for "contraction" to tell what the apostrophe shows in the sentence.**

C P **1.** We helped wash Dad's car.

C P **2.** We've always enjoyed helping him.

C P **3.** But today, it's a little too cold for car washing!

C P **4.** We should make sure the car's defroster works.

C P **5.** We set up a business in our neighbor's driveway.

C P **6.** Our neighbor said she won't charge us if we wash her car first.

C P **7.** But she said that today's the day to do it.

C P **8.** I guess a business can't always wait for a sunny day.

C P **9.** We asked Dad if he'd like to help us.

C P **10.** We would've paid him, too.

C P **11.** Dad said that we had already washed our family's car.

C P **12.** Mom said she could hear my dad's laugh all the way down the hall.

B **What clues did you use to decide if a word was possessive or a contraction?**

_____

_____

Advantage Grammar Grade 5 © 2005 Creative Teaching Press

Name _____

C Read the advertisements below. Cross out any apostrophes that should not be there. If the apostrophe is used correctly, circle whether it indicates a possessive or a contraction.

Visit Dan's Do-It-Yourself Dog Washing   C P
Is your dog's odor like his breath?   C P
Can't stand it any longer?   C P
We take all dog's here!   C P

The Cat's Meow   C P
Every cat owner knows that we're the actual pet!   C P
Please your master—get kitty's litter and everything else here.   C P
Please your kitty and the world is your's!   C P

DVD's For Sale   C P
There's not a movie missing from our shelves!   C P
Get all you favorite's here!   C P
You won't find better deals anywhere else!   C P

Don't Eat Carbs Store   C P
Do you have weakness's for carbohydrates?   C P
The number of carbs in your groceries is anyone's guess.   C P
Buy your food here so you won't have to guess anymore!   C P

Laura's Laser Tag   C P
Want more fun with your friend's?   C P
Need something new to do for Grandpa's birthday?   C P
It doesn't get any more fun than at Laser Tag! C P

Name _____

Improving Paragraphs

 When writing, start with a rough draft just to get your ideas down.

> An urban legend is a rumor that's been floating around. No one knows who started them and they usually happened to a "friend of a friend." Every so often the old urban legend about alligators in the sewers of New York pop up again. Before you pass on information, check out the source first. A lot of times the legend sounds so silly "it just has to be true because you can't make this stuff up!"

Then be prepared to change the order of sentences, to improve your word choices, to add transitions, and to leave parts out. Rewrite your draft to make your paragraph better.

> An urban legend is a rumor that is untrue, but continues to be told. Many of these legends sound so silly it's hard to believe some one would invent the story. One popular urban legend is that alligators live in the sewers of New York City. Before you pass on a rumor, check out the source first!

 Rewrite the paragraph below.

Some people think that German chocolate cake comes from Germany. An American invented the recipe for the chocolate used in the cake. His name was Sam German. The chocolate was called "German's Sweet Chocolate." Over the years, the apostrophe s has been dropped. Now people think that the chocolate and the cake was invented in Germany.

_____

_____

_____

_____

_____

_____

 Advantage Grammar Grade 5 © 2005 Creative Teaching Press

Name _____

B Rewrite the paragraphs below. Change the order, use better words, add transitions, and leave out parts that are repeated or unnecessary.

One urban legend is that certain snack cakes can last forever. Everyone knows the disappointment of opening a bag of food to find it hard or moldy. The legend says that these snack cakes never go bad. People say that they have so many chemicals that they last forever. The plastic wrap also keeps it from going bad.

_____

_____

_____

_____

_____

_____

_____

Actually these snack cakes will go bad after twenty-five days. This is still longer than other food. The company that makes the snack cakes says that they last longer because they don't use any dairy products. Food that uses dairy products goes bad quicker. Just think about the last time you smelled spoiled milk in your refrigerator or you had to cut off a piece of moldy cheese.

_____

_____

_____

_____

_____

_____

_____

Name _____

 Editing your work is an important step in the writing process. Many tests ask you to show what you know about editing.

A **Kayla wrote a report about an urban legend. Help her analyze and edit her report. Read the report and answer the questions that follow.**

The Potato Chip

1) The potato chip was actually invented by mistake. 2) George Crum, who was a head chef, worked at a restaurant in Saratoga Springs, New York. 3) One customer didn't never like his French fries and sent them back to the kitchen. 4) He complained that the cook's fries were "too thick and soggy" and "not salty enough." 5) Crum was'nt happy. 6) He decided to give his' customer exactly what he wanted. 7) This chef was insulted!

8) Crum cut potatoes as thin as possible, fried them until they were brown, and poured salt on them. 9) Then the chef brought the "potato crunche" to the customer, who loved them. 10) Soon everyone wanted the potatoe's. 11) They were known as "Saratoga chips" because they came from Saratoga Springs.

1. Rewrite sentence 3 to use only one negative word.

   _____

   _____

2. List the three words that use an apostrophe incorrectly and write the correct form of the words. _____

3. Does the apostrophe in the word *didn't* indicate a contraction or a possessive?

   _____

4. List the numbers of three sentences which have no dependent clauses. _____

5. What sentences could you move in the first paragraph to improve the paragraph? Where should the sentence be? _____

   _____

Advantage Grammar Grade 5 © 2005 Creative Teaching Press

B **Help Kayla revise and edit the rest of her report.**

12) The rest of the story about potato chips isn't as funny, but it is interesting. 13) Mr. Crum opened his own restaurant, where he put his "Saratoga chips" on every table. 14) It didn't take much time before everyone in the New England states were eating his invention. 15) A salesman from the South, who was named Herman Lay, discovered the chips and began selling them from his car to grocery stores.

16) The company that made the chips for Mr. Lay started having problems. 17) So Mr. Lay bought the company. 18) He could sell his potato chips all over the country. 19) So it's to George Crum and Herman Lay that we can give thanks for the most popular snack food in America!

1. Which word is a contraction in sentence 12, and what does it stand for?

   _____

2. Write a dependent clause from above that is in the middle of a sentence.

   _____

3. How could you change sentence 18 to improve the paragraph?

   _____

4. Write the independent clause in sentence 16.

   _____

5. Rewrite one sentence from the report changing it into a negative sentence.

   _____

   _____

6. Which sentence has two independent clauses and no dependent clause? _____

7. Which contraction is also a negative? What does the word stand for?

   _____

8. Write a sentence about the paragraph using a possessive word.

   _____

   _____

Name _____

48

Take a Test Drive

Fill in the bubble beside the correct answer.

Ryan wrote a report about the history of another popular dish. Help him analyze and edit his report. Read the report and answer the questions that follow.

Chop Suey

1) Do you like to eat Chinese food? 2) I do. 3) My family probably has Chinese takeout every week. 4) One item on the menu is chop suey. 5) But unlike other foods on the menu, the restaurant's recipe never could not have come from China. 6) The dish was an American's invention. 7) There are several stories about who invented it and why. 8) But most legends agree that Chinese-Americans created chop suey. 9) Besides that, the only other part of the food that is Chinese is the name – it means "odds and ends" in Chinese. 10) The funniest thing is that, in China, some restaurants serve what they call "American Chop Suey."

1. Which is NOT true about sentence 6?
   Ⓐ It does not have any dependent clauses.
   Ⓑ It has one independent clause.
   Ⓒ The word *American's* means "American has."
   Ⓓ The word *American's* is possessive.

2. Which sentence adds to the main idea of the history of chop suey?
   Ⓕ sentence 1   Ⓗ sentence 3
   Ⓖ sentence 2   Ⓙ sentence 5

3. What needs to be changed in sentence 5?
   Ⓐ The apostrophe needs to be taken out of the word *restaurant's*.
   Ⓑ It should be moved to the end of the paragraph.
   Ⓒ The word *never* should be taken out.
   Ⓓ Nothing, the sentence is perfect.

4. What is true about sentence 8?
   Ⓕ It does not have a dependent clause.
   Ⓖ It does not have an independent clause.
   Ⓗ "But most legends agree" is the dependent clause.
   Ⓙ "that Chinese-Americans created chop suey" is the dependent clause.

Read Ryan's paragraph about one of the legends about the invention of chop suey. Then answer the questions that follow.

11) One legend about chop suey involves a famous ambassador. 12) An ambassador's a person who represent his country around the world. 13) Li Hung-Chang was a very good ambassador from China who visited the United States. 14) Legends say that the ambassador's chef invented chop suey for him here.

15) Some legends say that the ambassador did not feel well. 16) He had eaten too much rich food while visiting Americans. 17) Chop suey is bland, so his' chef said that it would be better for his tummy.

18) Other legends say that the ambassador wanted his chef to make a dish that both Americans and Chinese would like. 19) Chinese food either had too much spice or too many strange vegetables for Americans. 20) So the new dish didn't have either one.

5. Which sentence has a possessive word using the apostrophe correctly?
   Ⓐ sentence 12   Ⓒ sentence 17
   Ⓑ sentence 14   Ⓓ sentence 20

6. What is true about the phrase "that the ambassador's chef invented chop suey for him here" in sentence 14?
   Ⓕ It is an independent clause.
   Ⓖ The word *ambassador's* means "the ambassador is."
   Ⓗ It is a dependent clause that completes the predicate.
   Ⓙ It is a dependent clause that makes up the subject.

7. Which sentence would most improve the paragraph it is in?
   Ⓐ Legend's say that the ambassador's chef invented chop suey for him here.
   Ⓑ Some legends say that the ambassador did not feel well because he had eaten too much rich food while visiting Americans.
   Ⓒ Chinese food had neither too much spice nor too many strange vegetables for Americans.
   Ⓓ So the new dish didn't have neither one.

8. What is NOT true about sentence 20?
   Ⓕ It has one independent clause.
   Ⓖ The phrase "So the new dish" is a dependent clause.
   Ⓗ The word *didn't* is a contraction for "did not."
   Ⓙ The word *didn't* makes the sentence negative.

Name _____

Practice Test

Read the paragraphs and answer the questions.

1) My family went to the movies together last night. 2) First we crowded into the car and drove to the theater. 3) Then we got out and stood in line for tickets. 4) When we got to the front of the line, we realized one thing: we hadn't agreed on a movie yet! 5) We had to go back to the end of the line while we decided what to see. 6) We almost missed the 800 movie!

1. Which statement is NOT true about sentence 1?

Ⓐ The verb is past tense.

Ⓑ The verb is irregular because went is a form of go.

Ⓒ The words "My family" is the subject of the sentence.

Ⓓ The word to should have a colon (:) after it.

2. Which sentence is the topic sentence?

Ⓕ sentence 1

Ⓖ sentence 2

Ⓗ sentence 4

Ⓙ sentence 6

3. How would you make this paragraph better?

Ⓐ Make the word drove into drives.

Ⓑ Take the colon out of sentence 4.

Ⓒ Take out the second sentence altogether

Ⓓ Add a colon to the time to make 8:00.

4. What is true about the paragraph?

Ⓕ It is structured: by topic sentence, details, closing sentence.

Ⓖ It is structured by time order.

Ⓗ Sentence 6 is a sentence fragment.

Ⓙ Sentence 4 is a run-on sentence.

5. Which rewritten sentence uses an emphatic verb?

Ⓐ My family was going to the movies together last night.

Ⓑ We had not agreed on a movie yet!

Ⓒ We went back to the end of the line.

Ⓓ We almost did miss the 8:00 movie!

6. Which is the best way to write the title of the movie they saw?

Ⓕ "The Superheroes"

Ⓖ The Superheroe's

Ⓗ The Superheroes

Ⓙ *The Superheroes*

Advantage Grammar Grade 5 © 2005 Creative Teaching Press

1) Maya and Andrew are friends. 2) They like to tell jokes to each other. 3) Andrew knows that Maya espeshally likes animal jokes. 4) "Who is a penguin's favorite relative?" asked Andrew. 5) "Let me see," said Maya. "That must be Aunt-Arctica!" 6) "Who is the penguins' leader?" asked Andrew. 7) "The first one to the ice floe," answered Maya. 8) "No," said Andrew. "It's Admiral Byrd."

7. Which word has a silent letter?

Ⓐ they   Ⓒ knows
Ⓑ each   Ⓓ animal

8. Which change is correct?

Ⓕ Take out the words *like to* so there is only one verb in sentence 2.
Ⓖ Change the word *espeshally* to *especially*.
Ⓗ Move the question mark outside of the quotation marks.
Ⓙ Change the word *it's* to *its*.

9. What is true about the quote in sentence 7?

Ⓐ It is a sentence fragment because it does not have a verb.
Ⓑ The comma should be outside of the quotation marks.
Ⓒ It should be underlined instead of in quotation marks.
Ⓓ Floe is misspelled.

10. Which combination of sentences 1 and 2 is best?

Ⓕ Maya and Andrew are friends they like to tell jokes to each other.
Ⓖ Maya and Andrew are friends but they like to tell jokes to each other.
Ⓗ Maya and Andrew are friends: they like to tell jokes to each other.
Ⓙ Maya and Andrew are friends who like to tell jokes to each other.

11. What is NOT true about sentence 3

Ⓐ It is a compound sentence.
Ⓑ "Andrew knows" is an independent clause.
Ⓒ "that Maya espeshally likes animal jokes" is an independent clause.
Ⓓ "that Maya espeshally likes animal jokes" completes the predicate.

12. Which list of names is in alphabetical order?

Ⓕ Maya, Andrew, Arctica, Byrd
Ⓖ Andrew, Byrd, Maya, Arctica
Ⓗ Artica, Andrew, Byrd, Maya
Ⓙ Andrew, Arctica, Byrd, Maya

Practice Test

To: 2012grad@blingbling.com
From: spider@vanline.net
Date: Nov. 8, 2004
Subject: visit

Hi, J.J,
1) My mom said that we can schedule a visit. 2) So let me know when you'll be home, and I'll call you than. 3) I can't hardly wait until you can come! 4) Playing computer games will be most fun in person. 5) You can use my dad's computer while I use his' laptop.

Later, Spiderman

13. Which word shows ownership and uses the apostrophe correctly?
   Ⓐ you'll   Ⓒ dad's
   Ⓑ can't   Ⓓ his'

14. What should be changed in sentence 2?
   Ⓕ Move the apostrophe in I'll to Il'l.   Ⓗ It should be split into two sentences.
   Ⓖ Change the word *than* to *then*.   Ⓙ Nothing, the sentence is perfect.

15. Which is the best way to write sentence 3?
   Ⓐ I can't hardly wait until you can come!   Ⓒ I can hardly wait until you can come!

   Ⓑ I can't hardly never wait until you can come!   Ⓓ I can hardly wait until you can't come!

16. What change should be made in sentence 4?
   Ⓕ Add an apostrophe to the word *games*.   Ⓗ Change *most fun* to *funnest*.
   Ⓖ Add a comma after the word *games*.   Ⓙ Change *most fun* to *more fun*.

17. What kind of word is *hardly* in sentence 3?
   Ⓐ An adverb modifying *can wait*   Ⓒ A transition
   Ⓑ An adjective modifying *games*   Ⓓ A preposition

18. Which word does NOT add the *–ing* ending correctly?
   Ⓕ scheduling   Ⓗ waiting
   Ⓖ calling   Ⓙ useing

                       Advantage Grammar Grade 5 © 2005 Creative Teaching Press

Read the review Stephanie wrote about a computer game. Then answer the questions.

     1) I tried the new computer game, "Popcorn Wars." 2) My friend, who is also really good at computer games, and I played it together. 3) Then I also played it alone. 4) "Popcorn Wars" was a fun game. 5) Some of the game was hard. 6) Some of it was easy. 7) One reward in the adventure was getting more salt on your popcorn! 8) We thought that was the funnier part of the game. 9) Then we played our favorite game, "Lambcake Strikes Again."

19. Which phrase is an appositive?
    (A) new computer game
    (B) who is also really good at computer games
    (C) some of the game
    (D) getting more salt on your popcorn!

20. Which is the best combination of sentences 5 and 6?
    (F) Some of the game was hard some of it was easy.
    (G) Some of the game was hard: some of it was easy.
    (H) Some of the game was hard but some of it was easy.
    (J) Some of the game was hard, and some of it was easy.

21. Which phrase is NOT a prepositional phrase?
    (A) the new computer game
    (B) in the adventure
    (C) of it
    (D) on your popcorn

22. Which sentence should be taken out of the paragraph?
    (F) sentence 1
    (G) sentence 3
    (H) sentence 7
    (J) sentence 9

23. What should be changed in sentence 8?
    (A) Change *was* to *were*.
    (B) Change *funnier* to *more funny*.
    (C) Change *funnier* to *funniest*.
    (D) Nothing, the sentence is perfect.

24. Why shouldn't sentences 2 and 3 be combined?
    (F) Because they are not related.
    (G) Because it would be too long.
    (H) Because they do not have the same subject.
    (J) Because they are both independent clauses.

Answer Key

Lesson 1
A
1. present
2. past
3. present
4. past
5. future
6. past
7. future
8. present

B

Present Tense	Past Tense	Future Tense
fly	flew	will fly
form	formed	will form
grow	grew	will grow
walk	walked	will walk
ask	asked	will ask
see	saw	will see
wash	washed	will wash
know	knew	will know

C
Present: fly, form, walk, ask, see
Past: grew, blew, saw, washed

```
H  A  B  M  X  S  O  A
W  A  L  K  L  A  N  S
A  K  E  S  A  W  E  K
S  I  W  C  T  A  R  P
H  L  A  F  L  Y  N  S
E  A  R  O  R  S  N  E
D  T  G  R  E  W  B  E
V  I  U  M  Z  Q  P  A
```

Lesson 2
A
1. form
2. cools
3. build
4. rise
5. erodes
6. wears
7. creates
8. shape

B
Sentences will vary.

C (sample answers)
1. treads – present
2. blew – past
3. will move – future
4. causes – present
5. form – present
6. had – past
7. will burst – future
8. fell – past
9. will bend – future
10. made – past

Lesson 3
A
1. A glacier is formed by snow, ice, air, and dirt.
2. Snowflakes and snow grains.
3. Packed snow slowly becomes ice.
4. Some glaciers are ice sheets.
5. Ice sheets covered the land completely.

B
1. Glaciers occur in polar regions or high altitudes, because they are cold.
2. Part of a glacier sometimes breaks off, and then it forms an iceberg.
3. Sometimes a glacier fills a valley between mountains so it is called a valley glacier.
4. Part of the glacier is melting, and another part is freezing.
5. Sometimes part of the glacier covers the land, yet another part floats in the ocean.

C
1. CS (line after "move,")
2. SS
3. SS
4. SS
5. SS
6. CS (line after "land,")
7. SS
8. SS
9. CS (line after "glacier")
10. SS

Lesson 4
A
1. after "warning"
2. after "words"
3. after "continents"
4. after "earthquakes"
5. after "disasters"
6. after "words"
7. after "alive"
8. 4:00, 7:30

B
From: Jacob <tremor@ ethquk.com>
To: <programming@infotv.com>

Subject: movie times
Date: Mon, Sept 6, 2004 4:36

Dear Programming Department:
I watched Channel 5 on Friday night and saw the end of "San Francisco: Aftermath of an Earthquake."

C
From: <programming@infotv.com>
To: Jacob <tremor@ethquk.com>
Subject: Re: movie times
Date: (Date and reply will vary.)

Lesson 5
A
Underline the first and last sentences. Circle the rest of the sentences.

B
Paragraphs will vary.

C
1, 5, 2, 3, 4

D
Paragraphs will vary.

Advantage Grammar Grade 5 © 2005 Creative Teaching Press

Lesson 6

A

social, erosion, artificial, usually, commercial, financial, precious, occasion, organizations, cautious, pollution, shame, appreciate, suggestions, tension, nation

B

Other words may vary.
sh: shame
su: usually
ci: precious, commercial, artificial, financial, appreciate, social
ti: nation, suggestions, cautious, pollution, organizations
si: erosion, tension, occasion

C

Paragraphs will vary.

Lesson 7

A

1. sentence 1
2. After an eruption, the ash in the sky makes something beautiful: a sunset.
3. sentence 6
4. sentence 7 Scientists name three main shapes of volcanoes, but they know several other shapes that are more unusual.

B

1. explosion
2. shook, eruption, ash, eruptions, shaped, reshaped
3. sentence 3
4. At 8:32 AM on May 18, a huge earthquake shook the swollen part.
5. The volcanic mudflow poured down the mountain doing much damage. It destroyed roads and bridges and ripped trees from their roots.
6. sample verbs: began, blew, created, shaped

Lesson 8

1. D   5. C
2. H   6. J
3. C   7. C
4. G   8. F

Lesson 9

A

1. past: was leaking   5. present: am settling
2. past: were returning   6. present: am finding
3. past: was planning   7. present: is learning
4. past: were living   8. past: were creating

B

1. did survive
2. did serve
3. did try
4. do believe
5. did share

C

Sentences will vary.

Lesson 10

A

1. were
2. brought
3. except
4. have
5. loose

B

1. saw   6. there
2. seen   7. scene
3. leave   8. there
4. its   9. You're
5. their   10. It's

Lesson 11

A

1. S   6. F
2. F   7. S
3. F   8. F
4. S   9. F
5. F   10. F

B

1. In 1607, English businessmen sailed to what is now Virginia to settle there. There they would look for gold and other riches they had heard were in this "New World."
2. The settlers looked for a place that would be easy to defend from other gold-diggers. So they sailed up a river to find a beautiful, secure area of land large enough to hold all 104 men.
3. Although the land was good for defense, the Jamestown settlement had other problems. For example, mosquitoes passed deadly diseases to the men.
4. Also, natives often attacked the settlers. Finally, some settlers could not—or would not—hunt for food.

Lesson 12

A

1. Benjamin Franklin spoke of actions being better than words when he said, "Well done is better than well said."
2. Although he led the military in the Revolutionary War, George Washington himself stated, "My first wish is to see this plague of mankind, war, banished from the earth."
3. Patrick Henry spoke the first declaration of independence when he said, "Give me liberty or give me death!"
4. As the colonies decided to fight for their independence, Thomas Paine said. "These are the times that try men's souls."
5. The great Thomas Jefferson once said, "Friendship is precious, not only in the shade, but in the sunshine of life."
6. British writer Samuel Johnson stated, "Hope is necessary in every condition."
7. Early American poet Anne Bradstreet wrote, "If we had no winter, the spring would not be so pleasant."

Answer Key

B
1. "I'm a great believer in luck," said Thomas Jefferson. "I find the harder I work, the more I have of it."
2. "There never was a good knife made of bad steel," Ben Franklin wrote.
3. "Take care that you never spell a word wrong," Thomas Jefferson once told his daughter. "Always before you write a word, consider how it is spelled, and, if you do not remember, turn to a dictionary."
4. "Men are born to succeed, not fail," Henry David Thoreau said.
5. "We are inclined to believe those whom we do not know because they have never deceived us," said Samuel Johnson.

C
Sentences will vary.

Lesson 13
A
1. before, Jamestown, isle
2. Lane, would, take, charge
3. arrived, autumn, late
4. Native, sometimes
5. kidnapped, natives, stole
6. islanders, would
7. came, returned, stayed
8. knows, palms
9. were, talked, disappeared
10. some, believe, Roanoke, moved, natives, some, believe, natives, killed

B (sample words in parentheses)
consonant y: yet (yes)
long e: colony, story, many (very)
long i: rhyme (cry)
short i: mysterious (bicycle)

Lesson 14
A
Underline the first sentence. Choose: The French people explored North America, then they returned home.

B
Paragraphs will vary.

C
Underline the first sentence. Cross out: The Spanish army was the colonists' ally during the Revolutionary War. Choose: Spanish settlers lived in islands in the Caribbean, such as Cuba and Puerto Rico.

D
Underline the first sentence. Cross out: Native Americans sometimes shared the land and sometimes chased out new settlers. Choose: People from Northern Europe and countries such as Denmark and Holland, also moved to America.

Lesson 15
A
1. sentence 2 – were becomong
2. sentence 3 – Soon the settlements became towns. Then later, some towns became cities.
3. sentence 1, their
4. But Henry David Thoreau said, "What is most interesting for the history of the Northwest are the natural facts, which are without date."

B
1. gained, people, could, become, state
2. than – then
3. sentence 12, was going on
4. underline sentence 9
5. Choose: The territory was the area east of the Mississippi River, and between the Ohio River and the Great Lakes.

Lesson 16
1. C	5. B
2. G	6. G
3. D	7. A
4. H	8. H

Lesson 17
A (adjective – noun)
1. low – shrubs, young – trees, forest – floor
2. low – light, higher – branches
3. soft – moss, green – moss, slow-growing – fungus
4. scaly – lizards, sky-high branches
5. silent – beetles, fallen – logs
6. shy – deer, velvety – antlers, green – leaves
7. playful – squirrels, precious – nuts
8. bright – birds, black – snakes, hollow – tree
9. colorful – wildflowers, enough – sunlight
10. tender – branches

B
1. many
2. rural, urban
3. small, large
4. wild, native
5. prairie

C
Sentences will vary.

Lesson 18
A
1. v	5. adv
2. v	6. v
3. adj, adv	7. v
4. adj	8. adv

B
1. brightly
2. dully
3. often
4. tightly
5. slowly

Advantage Grammar Grade 5 © 2005 Creative Teaching Press

C

```
Y  N  O  W  S  L  O  T
R  A  F  T  W  S  W  S
B  C  R  I  G  H  T  H  I
   M  I  N  A  F  A  R  L
Y  U  N  A  L  G  R  D  L
L  C  A  L  L  O  L  L  Y
K  H  L  L  Y  W  Y  T  T
C  Q  G  E  T  E  E  S
I  L  L  G  E  T  R  M  T
U  P  U  I  V  E  R  A  M
Q  T  T  V  E  R  N  Y  N
A  T  I  E  R  P  L  Y
O  S  K  I  P  P  L  S  N
```

adverbs: now, very, still, quite, quickly, many, much, sweetly, hardly, finally

other words: fast, bright, pretty, grow, ill, get, skip, lots, puts, raft, tie, tag, mar

Lesson 19

A
1. second
2. first
3. second
4. first
5. second
6. first
7. second
8. second

B
1. Cooler grasslands that do not have trees at all are called prairies.
2. Most grassland plants have thin leaves so they don't get burned by the sun.
3. Most of the plant is underground to avoid sun and wind.
4. American prairies are called the Wheat Belt because so much grain is grown there.
5. Besides being used for food, prairie grass is good for grazing animals.

C
Sentences will vary.

Lesson 20

A and B

The sheriff nodded then spoke to an unseen person under his desk. "Liak, you can stay if you stay quiet," said Sheriff Okituk. "Now, what can I do for you gentlemen?"

"We're having a misunderstanding over a deed," Tuma explained.

Cloud held up a piece of paper and said, "Oil has just been discovered on my family's land."

"Stop right there," said Tuma. "It's my family's land, not yours. I could have proved it until my deed was stolen last week."

"I know these parts pretty well, and I know who owns what," said the Sheriff. "Just tell me where the oil was discovered and I'll know who it belongs to."

"But it's not around here," said Tuma. "It's up north—in the tundra."

"Is it even colder up there than it is here?" asked a voice from under the desk.

"Quiet, little one," warned Sheriff Okituk.

But Cloud laughed and said, "That's right, it's even colder! And you have to be careful the polar bears don't eat you up. Why, my grandfather who owned the land talked about seeing penguins being eaten whole by a bear!"

"Oh, Daddy," said Liak, still under the desk, "now you know who's lying!"

Her father laughed and said "Yes, even my little girl knows that penguins only live in the southern part of the world!"

C
1. "Why did the walrus cross the water?" asked Baral.
   "I don't know," said Sedna. "Why?"
   Baral answered, "To get to the other tide."
2. "I've got a joke, too," said Sedna. "What did the sea say to the iceberg?"
   "You're so cool," guessed Baral.
   "No," answered Sedna, "It didn't say anything. It just waved."
3. "What is a baby grasshopper after it is six days old?" asked Sedna.
   "Seven days old," said Baral.
4. "What's a snowy owl's favorite salad?" asked Baral.
   "Let me guess," said Sedna. "Does it have iceberg lettuce?"
5. "Here's one more joke about the tundra," said Baral. "What do you call a gigantic polar bear?"
   "Nothing," said Sedna. "I wouldn't call it—I would run away!"

Lesson 21

A
1. known
2. formed
3. grows
4. finds
5. building
6. producing

B

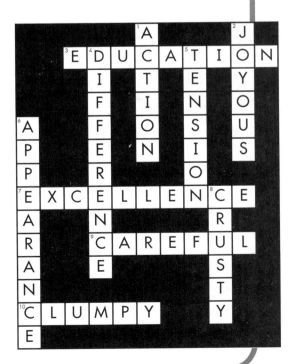

Answer Key

Lesson 22

A
Underline the first sentence. Cross out: Plants don't eat like animals do, but they still need energy. Check the first sentence.

B
Underline the first sentence. Cross out: The sun is in the center of our solar system. Check the second sentence.

C
Put an X by the second, fifth, and eighth sentences.

Lesson 23

A
1. Underline sentence 1.
2. facts
3. comma after the word *says*
4. wrongly – verb; only – verb
5. Rain forests are actually forests that get a lot of rain year round.
6. Cross out sentence 7

B
1. "Where else is there to live?" asked Fajar.
2. more – orangutan, protected – areas
3. "I think they only live on Borneo," wrote Fajar. "But you must have animals there that we don't."

Lesson 24
1. A   5. C
2. J   6. F
3. C   7. D
4. H   8. G

Lesson 25

A
1. and
2. or
3. (and) camping, hiking, and skiing
4. (or) old mining towns, the mountains, or the
5. or
6. nor
7. and
8. (or) Mountain States, the Southwest,

B
1. and
2. nor
3. but
4. (or) car, plane, train, or boat
5. and

C
1. Rivers are used for trade, travel, food, and water.
2. The Mississippi's waters come from Lake Itasca and from rivers that flow into it.
3. The Missouri River, Ohio River, White River, and many other rivers flow into the Mississippi.

4. Neither the Colorado River nor the Rio Grande flow into the Mississippi.
5. People fish for carp, perch, and bass in the Mississippi.

Lesson 26

A
1. Massachusetts
2. the first state to have lifeguards
3. New York City
4. a 2,100-mile footpath
5. or "red island"
6. Delmar
7. the official state beverage
8. "the sweetest place on Earth"
9. or "green"
10. New Hampshire

B (appositive – noun)
1. Nathan Hale – famous soldier
2. the Peach State – Georgia
3. made of spongy Palmetto logs – a Revolutionary War fort
4. once part of Massachusetts – Maine
5. Theodore and Franklin Roosevelt – Presidents

C
Sentences will vary.

Lesson 27

A
1. DC, IC
2. IC, DC
3. DC, IC
4 IC, DC
5. DC, IC

B
Sentences will vary.

Lesson 28

A (conjunction in parentheses)
1. (for) devastating,
2. (or) Stadium,
3. (and) water,
4. (and) Missouri,
5. (but) states,

B
1. so
2. but

C
1. Detroit, Michigan, is called "Motor City" and also "Motown."
3. Michigan is called the Great Lake State, but it does not touch Lake Ontario.
5. Ohio is considered part of the Midwest, but it is in the easternmost third of the country.
6. We had to drive through Indiana on the way to Illinois, so we stopped in Indianapolis to sightsee.

Advantage Grammar Grade 5 © 2005 Creative Teaching Press

7. We could visit the Mall of America in Minnesota, or we could see a Minnesota Twins ball game.
8. Wisconsin is the dairy capital of the U.S, for it produces more milk than any other state.

Lesson 29
A
1. Connecticut
2. Idaho
3. Maine
4. Vermont
5. Arizona
6. New Jersey

B
1. Florida, New York, Washington
2. Colorado, Georgia, Hawaii
3. Nevada, New Mexico, Rhode Island
4. North Carolina, South Carolina, South Dakota
5. Ohio, Oklahoma, Oregon

C
Florida, Kentucky, Michigan, Mississippi, Montana, North Dakota, Oregon, Tennessee, Texas, Utah

D

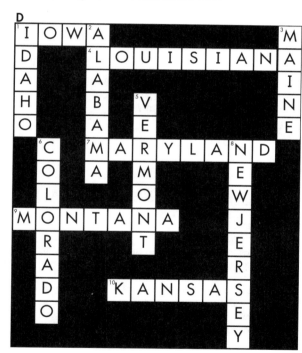

Lesson 30
A
1. Samoa certainly has an interesting and unique history.
2. The Midway Islands are a territory of the U.S.A.

B Sample sentences:
1. The Virgin Islands are very small islands.
2. U.S. territories have several things in common.

Lesson 31
A
1. My family lived in Hawaii.
2. Oahu, Honolulu
3. Hawaii, Kahoolawe, Kauai, Lanai, Maui, Molokai, Niihau, Oahu
4. The volcanoes don't erupt in violent explosions, but the hot lava is still dangerous.

B
1. (sample sentence) Less than fifty years old, Hawaii is the youngest state.
2. Los Angeles Airport – closest airport
3. People in Hawaii like to swim, surf, snorkel, and boat.
4. always, is, it, means, that, this, warm
5. sentence 15

Lesson 32
1. A
2. F
3. D
4. F
5. D
6. H
7. A
8. G

Lesson 33
A
1. on my calendar
2. in the cupboard
3. after school
4. to the library
5. with pockets
6. in the box
7. down the street
8. at each corner
9. according to my mom
10. throughout the day
11. toward the yard
12. until today

B
with my umbrella, on my shoulder, under the willow, in her big umbrella

C
Sentences will vary.

Lesson 34
A
1. lonelier
2. shorter
3. ugliest
4. fastest
5. brightest
6. sleepier
7. older
8. scarier
9. smarter
10. more afraid
11. longest

B (mistake – correction – reason)
1. more – most – compare more than 2 things
2. greatest – greater – compare 2 things
3. most – more – compare 2 things
4. dreadfuler – more dreadful – too long to add an ending
5. most – more – compare 2 things

Answer Key

Lesson 35

A

from, from there, until, but, for instance, since then

B
1. C
2. E
3. A
4. D
5. B

C

Paragraphs will vary.

Lesson 36

A
1. lose
2. since
3. whose
4. were
5. quiet
6. past
7. know
8. except
9. since
10. loose
11. passed
12. now
13. who's
14. quite

B

whose, now, lose, quite, passed, quiet, accept, know, Since, sense, loose, quite, where, Who's, except, passed

Lesson 37

A (sample sentences)
1. The Emperor loved to show off and most of all, to dress up.
2. Two fortune-hunters passing through the country heard about the Emperor's wealth and vanity.
3. The two men sneaked around the palace. They stole fancy clothes right off the drying line and then they dressed in the fanciest clothes.
4. The servants noticed the fancy clothes. They knew their ruler would be interested in buying more clothes, so they brought the "tailors" to see him.
5. The "tailors" bragged that their clothes had a special property, and said that anyone who did not deserve his position would not be able to see the clothes.

B (sample)

The "tailors" brought the final work to him, but the Emperor could not see anything. But since he did not want anyone to think he was unfit to be ruler, the Emperor said that he loved the new clothes. The lords and ladies also did not want to look bad, so they said that they loved the clothes too.

One "tailor" said that the Emperor should have a royal parade for all to see. The Emperor liked the idea of showing off and decided to have the parade. The "tailors" took their payment and left the land before the parade.

The Emperor started his parade. But no one could see his new clothes. Everyone was afraid, so all his subjects shouted praises and clapped for the new clothes. One little boy did not understand what was happening, for he could not see the clothes. He thought the Emperor looked silly.

The little boy shouted, "Look! The Emperor has no clothes!" Then the Emperor knew that he had been tricked and he was very embarrassed. He tried to find the "tailors" to punish them, but the "tailors" were already gone.

Lesson 38

A
1. <u>Biscuit</u>
2. "Chicken Little."
3. <u>The Apple Pie</u>
4. <u>The Times Journal</u>
5. "Locals Win Awards."
6. <u>Romeo</u>
7. "Rain, Rain, Go Away"
8. "Circle of Life" <u>The Lion King</u>
9. <u>Reader's Digest</u> "Humor in Uniform."
10. Aesop's <u>Fables</u> "The Tortoise and the Hare."
11. <u>Snow White</u> "Heigh-Ho."
12. "Bad News" <u>Charlotte's Web</u>

B

Titles will vary but should follow rules on page 78.

C

Sentences will vary.

Lesson 39

A
1. The Trumpet of the Swan, Charlotte's Web, Charlotte's Web, The Trumpet of the Swan, "Boston," The Swan
2. Sample (sentences 4 & 5): But I think <u>The Trumpet of the Swan</u> is more interesting because it seems real.
3. most – more
4. accept – except; quite – quiet

B
1. <u>The Trumpet of the Swan</u>, "Louie, Louie, Louie," <u>The Trumpet of the Swan</u>
2. new – knew
3. for one thing, but
4. Sample (sentences 20 & 21): All the songs are stupid and boring.
5. hilariouser – more hilarious, were – where
6. Should be two of the following: of the swan, for Christmas, of the book, for little kids, for one thing, of the movie, in the movie, in the book, from the book, on the shelf

Lesson 40
1. C
2. G
3. C
4. F
5. B
6. F
7. D
8. H
9. D

Advantage Grammar Grade 5 © 2005 Creative Teaching Press

Lesson 41

A

1. IC	7. IC
2. DC	8. IC
3. DC	9. DC
4. IC	10. DC
5. DC	11. IC
6. DC	12. DC

B

1. IC, DC	6. IC, DC
2. DC, IC	7. DC, IC
3. IC, DC	8. IC, DC
4. IC, DC	9. DC, IC
5. DC, IC	10. IC, DC

C (sample sentence)

I read each separately to see if it was a complete sentence.

Lesson 42

A

1. <u>Finally we could see</u> <u>why there was such a fuss.</u>
   DC   IC
2. <u>Standing in the middle of the crowd,</u> <u>there was a</u>
   DC   IC
   <u>volleyball net.</u>
3. <u>Although most teams have more players,</u> <u>each side had</u>
   DC   IC
   <u>only three players each.</u>
4. <u>I recognized one player,</u> <u>who was my neighbor.</u>
   DC   IC
5. <u>The players were sweating</u> <u>even though it was cool on</u>
   DC   IC
   <u>the beach.</u>
6. <u>Since there were so few players,</u> <u>each person got to</u>
   DC   IC
   <u>play a lot.</u>
7. <u>We loved watching</u> <u>how the players spiked the ball</u>
   IC   DC
   <u>over the net.</u>
8. <u>After watching the match,</u> <u>we all wanted to play, too!</u>
   DC   IC

B

1. (2) We sat in the stands, but actually we usually stood to cheer!
2. (1) <u>After we watched the game,</u> my friends and I played three-on-three.
3. (1) It was a lot of ground <u>that each player had to cover!</u>
4. (1) My friends wanted to see <u>what was going on at the park.</u>
5. (1) My sister, <u>who is very fast,</u> also came to play.
6. (1) Mom called to see <u>when we'd be home.</u>
7. (1) Some of us think <u>that we could play professionally.</u>
8. (2) Many athletes go straight into a major-league team after graduation, but others become professional by first playing for a minor-league team.

Lesson 43

A

1. We do not like online gaming.
2. My brother does not play against other people.
3. He is not good at some games.
4. I would rather not play a game in person.
5. I do not practice on my own before I go online.
6. It is not fun to talk with my friends online.
7. Last night I did not talk to my grandma online.
8. I do not think the phone is better than the computer.

B

```
R  N  Y  O  T  L  X  R  M  I
E  D  B  A  R  E  L  Y  L  O
V  E  C  R  E  F  P  H  E  R
E  P  A  E  H  A  R  D  L  Y
N  O  N  O  T  I  C  C  A  S
A  I  N  N  I  U  R  O  I  N
Z  R  O  P  E  O  L  U  R  G
R  N  T  U  N  A  B  L  E  J
E  Y  S  L  O  R  N  T  G  P
```

C

Sentences will vary.

Lesson 44

A

1. won't – will not	7. We're – we are
2. didn't – did not	8. couldn't – could not
3. would've – would have	9. there's – there is
4. he'd – he would	10. can't – cannot
5. He's – He is	11. It's – It is
6. you'll – you will	12. I'll – I will

B

1. wasn't	6. won't
2. we'd	7. hasn't
3. he'd	8. won't
4. it's	9. Let's
5. can't	10. you'll

C

Sentences will vary.

Lesson 45

A

1. P	7. C
2. C	8. C
3. C	9. C
4. P	10. C
5. P	11. P
6. C	12. P

B

Answers will vary

Answer Key

C

Dan's Do-It Yourself Dog Washing:
C. P, P, C, cross out

The Cat's Meow:
P, C, P, cross out

DVD's For Sale:
cross out, C, cross out, C

Don't Eat Carbs Store:
C, cross out, P, C

Laura's Laser Tag:
P, cross out, P, C

Lesson 46

A (sample paragraph)

Some people think that German chocolate cake comes from Germany. Actually, an American invented the recipe for the chocolate used in the cake. His name was Sam German, so the chocolate was called "German's Sweet Chocolate." Over the years, the apostrophe s has been dropped. Now many people think that the chocolate - and the cake - was invented in Germany.

B (sample paragraphs)

One urban legend is that certain snack cakes can last forever. The legend says that these snack cakes never go bad, they never get hard or moldy. People say that they have so many chemicals that they last forever.

Actually these snack cakes will go bad after twenty-five days. Still, this is longer than other food. The company that makes the snack cakes says that they last longer because they don't use any dairy products. Food that uses dairy products goes bad more quickly. The company also says that the plastic wrap also keeps it from going bad.

Lesson 47

A

1. One customer didn't like his French fries and sent them back to the kitchen.
2. was'nt – wasn't, his' – his, potatoe's – potatoes
3. contraction
4. 1, 5, 7, 10
5. Move sentence 7 to combine with sentence 5.

B

1. isn't – is not
2. who was named Herman Lay or that made the chips for Mr. Lay
3. Add the transition "Then"
4. The company started having problems
5. sample sentence 17: So Mr. Lay did not buy the company.
6. sentence 12
7. didn't – did not
8. Sentences will vary.

Lesson 48

1. C	5. B
2. J	6. H
3. C	7. B
4. J	8. G

Practice Test

1. D
2. F
3. D
4. G
5. D
6. J
7. C
8. G
9. A
10. J
11. A
12. J
13. C
14. G
15. C
16. J
17. A
18. J
19. B
20. J
21. A
22. J
23. C
24. G

Advantage Grammar Grade 5 © 2005 Creative Teaching Press